Research Reports Esprit

Project 9809 · SER · Volume 1

T0250584

Edited in cooperation with the European Commission, DGIII/F

Esprit, the Information Technology R&D Programme, was set up in 1984 as a co-operative research programme involving European IT companies, IT "user" organisations, large and small, and academic institutions. Managed by DGIII/F of the European Commission, its aim is to contribute to the development of a competitive industrial base in an area of crucial importance for the entire European economy. The current phase of the IT programme comprises the following eight domains: software technologies, technologies for components and subsystems, multimedia systems, long-term research, open microprocessor systems initiative, high-performance computing and networking, technologies for business processes, and integration in manufacturing.

The series *Research Reports Esprit* is helping to disseminate the many results – products and services, tools and methods, and international standards – arising from the hundreds of projects that have already been launched, involving thousands of researchers.

Springer
*Berlin
Heidelberg
New York
Barcelona
Budapest
Hong Kong
London
Milan
Paris
Santa Clara
Singapore
Tokyo*

S. Hallsteinsen   M. Paci (Eds.)

Experiences in Software Evolution and Reuse

Twelve Real World Projects

Springer

Volume Editors

Svein Hallsteinsen
SINTEF Telecom and Informatics
N-7034 Trondheim, Norway

Maddali Paci
TXT Ingegneria Informatica SpA
Via Socrate 41, I-20128 Milano, Italy

Cataloging-in-Publication Data applied for

Die Deutsche Bibliothek - CIP-Einheitsaufnahme

Experiences in software evolution and reuse / S. Hallsteinsen ; M.
Paci (ed.). - Berlin ; Heidelberg ; New York ; Barcelona ; Budapest ;
Hong Kong ; London ; Milan ; Santa Clara ; Singapore ; Paris ;
Tokyo : Springer, 1997
  (Research reports ESPRIT : Project 9809, SER ; Vol. 1)
  ISBN 3-540-62864-9

CR Subject Classification (1991): D.2.m

ISBN 3-540-62864-9 Springer-Verlag Berlin Heidelberg New York

Publication No. EUR 17765 EN of the
European Commission, Dissemination of Scientific and Technical Knowledge Unit,
Directorate-General Telecommunications, Information Market and Exploitation of Research,
Luxembourg.

Typesetting: Camera-ready by the editors
SPIN: 10576621   45/3142-543210 – Printed on acid-free paper

Preface

If implementing systematic reuse is risky, not doing it is even more risky. Trying systematic reuse unsuccessfully can cost precious time and resources and may make management sceptical of trying it again. But if your competitors do it successfully and you do not, you may lose market share and possibly an entire market.
    W. B. Frakes and S. Isoda, 1994

Software companies today are faced with new and more challenging market pressures. In response to this challenge, they have to reduce the time-to-market with new or enhanced products, increase the diversity of products available to the customers, and enhance the standardisation and interoperability of the products.

At the same time, many companies carry the burden of large legacy systems, that have become too expensive to maintain and cannot sustain the demands of the marketing department for alterations, leading to business opportunities being lost [BEN95]. However the systems are very valuable and cannot be simply replaced because of the costs that such an operation entails. Simply replacing them may be too expensive because of the huge volumes of on-line data that must be converted, among other reasons.

Planned software evolution and reuse are approaches for dealing with such challenges. This book builds upon trial application of solutions for planned software evolution and reuse proposed by a handful of ESPRIT projects. Drawing on the results of these trial applications as well as from the analysis of reports of experiences in the same field available in the literature, the book addresses the challenge of providing managers with quantitative indications about the benefits of software evolution and reuse programs.

There are clear indications that software reuse programs tend to have the highest return on investment of any technology in the history of software engineering (about $30.00 returned for every $1.00 invested), but there are also many obstacles that need to be tackled in order to achieve such results, and among many clear success stories, there are also many failures. This book tries to provide a key to interpret the diversity of the results obtained in practice.

The lack of uniformity among the success stories with respect to such factors as application domain, type of software produced and programming language used in developing the applications certainly indicates that there does not exist any *a priori* bias against the enactment of a reuse-oriented approach and/or of an evolutionary approach in particular situations. The key to success is for each company to make the right choices based on pre-existing organisational, managerial, and technical texture and careful evaluation of the foreseen benefits against the new costs. To enable a correct approach for tackling all the different aspects entailed by a reuse program, a chapter of the book outlines relevant organizational, managerial, and technological approaches to prototypical scenarios and problems.

If after reading the SER book you are still not convinced one hundred per cent about the benefits of introducing software reuse in your own company, just consider again the citation opening this preface.

Origins

In its 3rd Framework Programme, the CEC funded several projects aiming at developing technology for software evolution and reuse. In order to sustain its support for this technology and its uptake by the European software industry, the CEC asked selected partners from these projects to participate in the Software Evolution and Reuse deployment plan, SER for short, aiming at promoting and deploying the software evolution and reuse solutions produced by the projects.

A major set of activities of the SER was to follow up and document trial applications of the proposed technologies, to demonstrate the scope, applicability, benefits, and costs of the proposed solutions, and to investigate possible synergies among them. This book draws from the experience collected in these experiments, complemented with related experience reported in the literature.

The SER consortium consisted of:

- Athens Technology Centre for the EUROBANQUET project;
- Bull SA, EP Frameworks, and Q-Labs for the REBOOT project;
- Sema Group sae for the EUROWARE and REBOOT project;
- SINTEF for the REBOOT and the Proteus projects;
- The Technology Broker for the RECYCLE project;
- TXT Ingegneria Informatica for both the EUROWARE and the REBOOT projects.

Overview

The material in this book is divided into two parts. Part one synthesises the experience collected in the SER experiments and compares it with other experience reported in the literature. First, Chapter 1 "The SER Approach" briefly introduces the concepts of software evolution and reuse, presents the solutions offered by the SER projects, and gives an overview of the SER experiments. Chapter 2 "Benefits of Software Evolution and Reuse" presents the promised benefits of Software

Evolution and Reuse programs and compares them with actual achievements in the SER experiments and in other projects reported in the literature.

Drawing from the experience collected in the SER experiments, Chapter 3 "Lessons Learned" presents four prototypical scenarios together with relevant experiences. The underlying idea is that the scenarios are typical enough that most software producing companies will find one that resembles their own situation, and that the lesson learned in solving organisational, managerial, and technological issues for the experiments presented in the book will be useful for experiments carried out in similar circumstances.

Part II "Application Experiment Reports" presents each application experiment in more detail, so as to let the reader into the detailed description of the application contexts, organisational peculiarities, managerial approaches, specific problems, and technical solutions adopted.

Acknowledgements

First we would like to mention the contributors in addition to the editors of application experiment reports reproduced in Part II: Bill Karakostas of UMIST contributed the report from the application of EUROBANQUET technology in XIOSbank, Jean-Marc Morel of Bull contributed the report on experience with REBOOT in the Bull Office Automation Division, Jacqueline Floch and Joe Gorman of SINTEF and Bjørn Gulla of the Norwegian University of Science and Technology contributed the reports on the experimentation with Proteus technology in Stentofon and GAREX. The reports on the application of the REBOOT methodology to application framework development in Ericsson were adapted by the editors from bigger reports written by Grace Bosson and Johan Larsson of EP Frameworks. Furthermore section 1 "The SER Approach" reuses many parts from the SER deliverable "Solutions for Software Evolution and Reuse" written by Nicky Sutton of the Technology Broker. Without these contributions this book would not have been possible.

Then we would like to thank Jean-Marc Morel and Alejando Moya, Project Manager and EC Project Officer respectively, of the SER project, for their efforts to have this work published, and Springer-Verlag for supporting this publication. Jean Marc Morel also provided numerous valuable comments and suggestions for improvements during the preparation of the book.

Finally, we are indebted to the reviewers of the SER project, Piero Bucci and Daniel Claude for their constructive criticism during the SER project reviews.

Table of Contents

Part I
Experiences

For 25 years software researchers have proposed improving software development and maintenance with new practices whose effectiveness is rarely, if ever backed up by hard evidence.

Norman Fenton, Shari Lawrence Pfleeger and Robert L. Glass, July 1994

1 The SER Approach

1.1 Introduction

The history of of Software Engineering could can be seen the constant quest for better control of costs, quality and development time.

The claim of this book is that software evolution and reuse are today an important leverage to improve SE, that is they open a new route to dramatically reduce software development costs, to enhance quality and to better answer the demands of the market for shorter tiime-to-market.

From a technical stand point, evolution and reuse are alternate solutions to a similar problem. Depending on the characteristics of the domain, of the organisation and of the applications at hand it may be more convenient to focus on the reuse of software components in new contexts, that is, focus on the so called Software Reuse, or to focus on reuse of entire applications through parameterisation, reconfiguration and continued development, that is, on Software Evolution.

In its 3rd Framework Programme, the CEC funded several projects aiming at developing technology for software evolution and reuse. In order to sustain its support for this technology and its uptake by the European software industry, the CEC asked selected partners from these projects to participate in the Software Evolution and Reuse deployment plan (SER), aiming at promoting and deploying the software evolution and reuse solutions produced by the projects.

A major set of activities of the SER was to follow up and document trial applications of the proposed technologies, to demonstrate the scope, applicability, benefits and costs of the proposed solutions, and to investigate possible synergies among them. This book builds on the experience gathered in these trial applications. The idea is that it will provide the management of software organisations which are potential users of the proposed technologies with information based on real life experience on which they can base decisions and planning of the introduction of corresponding solutions in their own organisation.

Only a thorough analysis of the specific organisational, managerial and technological context pertaining to the company can lead to the appropriate definition of a competitive company strategy and to the choice of the best suited approach. However, previous experience in similar situations and circumstances is valuable input to making the necessary decisions.

The technologies subject to experimentation were technologies proposed by ESPRIT projects REBOOT, PROTEUS, EUROBANQUET and EUROWARE.

REBOOT and PROTEUS are the two most general technologies which could be considered as the axes of this book, having the broadest scope. Both propose complete SER oriented development paradigms, with REBOOT biased towards software component reuse and Proteus biased towards evolving software products.

The other projects are either more specialised in their scope, or are backward looking - that is, they allow analysis of existing applications which could help extract reusable code for future development or evolution.

Together, the SER projects offer most of the benefits associated with software reuse and evolution.

This chapter briefly presents each technology and then discusses how they may complement each other in practice. A brief overview of the experiments conducted in the context of the SER project is then provided.

1.2   The Applied Technologies

1.2.1   REBOOT - Reuse Methodology Based on Object Oriented Techniques

REBOOT is an integrated methodology concerned with the wider organisational issues of reuse, as well as with technical aspects in the day to day implementation of reuse (for example guidelines for developing reusable components). The methodology involves auditing the business to assess its suitability for reuse and to calculate the potential benefits of changing the processes. It then designs suitable processes and offers methodological and tool support for building, storing and classifying objects as well as support in reusing software assets within chosen domains of application, and is realised through systematic processes for developing products from a reusable asset base and adding assets to the base. It is applied in the context of the organisation and management of the company. Continued application of the REBOOT methods helps the organisation in all of the areas of company management, development process, product management and market and business development.

REBOOT distinguishes two essential processes in software reuse engineering: development *for* reuse and development *with* reuse.

In development *for* reuse, engineers identify what is potentially and profitably usable, the record related knowledge while designing, qualifying, constructing and classifying software artifacts for reuse in solutions other than those initially targeted. This includes domain analysis and domain modelling, which are key techniques to build reference models and a generic architecture usually implemented using object-oriented framework technology.

In development *with* reuse, engineers search for, evaluate adapt and integrate existing and appropriate knowledge, specifications, designs, codes, tests and documentation to deliver quality products in shorter time at lower costs. These

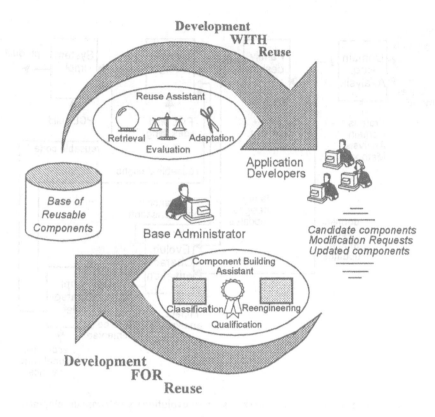

Fig. 1.1. The REBOOT view of organised reuse

assets can be searched for from the repository, from other systems developed in the company or from public bases accessed through networks.

The hinge around which the REBOOT methodology revolves is the Reuse Maturity Model (RMM) which has been developed to measure the extent to which a company succeeds in developing, maintaining and using all reusable assets at its disposal, and as a frame of reference for planning and following up reuse introduction and implementation programs.

1.2.2 Proteus - Support for Software Evolution

Proteus consists of several different strands of work, providing development and maintenance support for evolving systems. It focuses on improving the understanding of system evolution and supports this at various levels of abstraction. At the domain level, domain analysis methods and tools enable the building of domain models with predicted evolution. At the design level, the notion of system families plays a central role to represent sets of similar systems. Proteus proposes modifications to several popular design methods (HOOD, SDL, OORAM and MD) to encourage more emphasis on the role of system families in the design activities.

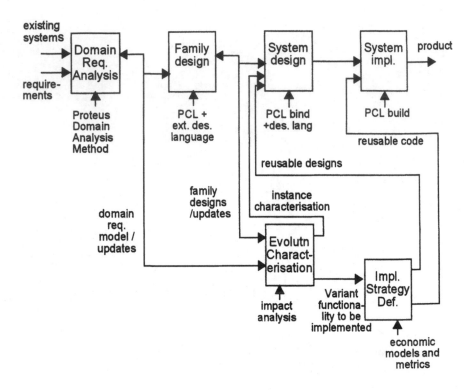

Fig. 1.2. Proteus conceptual framework to support evolutionary software development

At the implementation level, automatic code generators for the relevant design notations generating object oriented code are provided together with techniques for implementation description.

Central to the project are the Proteus Configuration Language (PCL) and tools which allow the structured modelling of evolving systems (both hardware and software). PCL was designed in order to help solve the problems which were associated with multiple versions and variants of systems that arise as products evolve, and a key characteristic of PCL is its ability to support this variability. Furthermore PCL supports modelling of the software building process. Together with a powerful notation for describing individual configurations and appropriate tools this allows for extensive automation of product building.

Support is also provided for describing and enacting process models for evolution. In addition the PPIS (Product and Process Information System) tool is used to record and design rationale information as products evolve.

1.2.3   EUROWARE - Enabling Reuse over Wide Areas

EUROWARE inherits many ideas from REBOOT, but focuses on the dissemination of reusable assets over modern networks. The intent is to develop technology supporting reuse in distributed organisations as well as a public market for reusable assets. The technology proposed by EUROWARE is a reusable asset model and a set of applications integrated with a WWW server supporting publication of and access to reusable assets complying with this model. The types of assets supported by the EUROWARE server are software components, methodology support documentation, references to literature, consultancy offers, training courses, customer history, available skills, reuse specific tools and agendas for specific reuse events.

The project has studied the component production process, producing methods and guidelines for the design and development of new components and the packaging of existing components for insertion into the component base. This includes the metrication and qualification of components.

In addition the EUROWARE tools provide process support for development with reuse, including the recording of actual uses of the assets in the base. This provides feedback to the management of the server and a natural forum for reusers to communicate with each other.

1.2.4   EUROBANQUET - Support for Effective Software Evolution in Banks

EUROBANQUET proposes a total approach to the evolution of software systems in banks. This approach begins with the specification of an external change, for instance a new EU or national legislation or change in the business environment, and ends with the detailed description of the required changes to the banks software systems, together with an estimation of the cost of implementing them. It is based on a common banking reference model, i.e. a model that is common across banks and can be customised for individual banks. The model consists of reusable banking objects corresponding to real banking entities, such as loan, loan application a.s.o. The advantages of this approach come from the ease of constructing new banking applications and the flexibility in modifying existing ones. The model relies on object oriented mechanisms for customisation for individual banks.

1.3   Comparison and Synergies

The technologies presented above overlap and complement each other in their support of the software engineering process, particularly with respect to the aspects of the process that support software evolution and reuse. This is illustrated in Fig. 1.3. Tthe rows of the presented table correspond to relevant aspects of the software engineering process, and each column, representing a particular project, indicates how the technology delivered by the project supports these aspects. The comparison is centred around 7 aspects:

- Introducing reuse into the organisation
- Development for reuse
- Storage of components

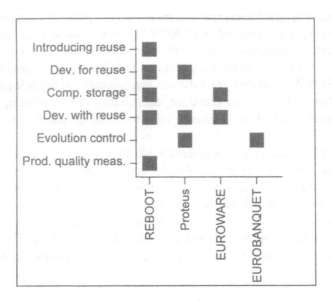

Fig. 1.3. Coverage of the SER technologies

- Development with reuse
- Evolution control and CM
- Product quality measurement

1.3.1 Introducing Reuse into the Organisation

Introducing reuse into the organisation is the first step in putting reuse principles into practice, and in this context is mainly concerned with management and organisational issues. Introducing reuse is not simply about finding an appropriate storage facility for code components, but also involves learning about what changes need to be made in an organisation and how to facilitate these changes.Reuse need s to be part of a long-term business strategy of the organisation, rather that just an effort to save money in the short term.

It is primarily REBOOT that provides support for this aspect. As well as supporting the cultural and organisational changes that need to be made, REBOOT helps in the mechanics of designing and implementing the reuse program. It provides methodologies to assess the organisation for its suitability to implement reuse, and then support the organisation in implementing reuse principles and practices.

1.3.2 Development for Reuse

This is the process of developing and preparing components such that they can be reused in future applications and contexts. Components typically include requirements analysis, design, interface specification, source code, tests and documentation. Development for reuse encompasses the design of components for maximum reusability as well as appropriate classification to facilitate effective retrieval in the development with reuse process.

REBOOT and PROTEUS both provide support for development for reuse. REBOOT provides methodological support by extending the ordinary development process by activities to:

- analyse the variability of requirements between different potential users of the components and identify commonalities
- analyse the costs and benefits of incorporating these requirements
- design the components with the appropriate generality and flexibility

Furthermore REBOOT provides support for reengineering, qualification and classification of reusable components, and packaging them in the REBOOT standard library format.

PROTEUS supports development for reuse by providing a method for domain analysis with special focus on identifying what is stable and what is varying in a domain. PROTEUS defines a rigorous process model for domain analysis defining a sequence of tasks to be carried out and the results to be produced, but does not offer much support on how to carry out the tasks. REBOOT on the other hand is more open about the process, but is stronger on practical guidelines for the work that has to be done in the various activities. Both use OMT as their primary object oriented modelling technique, but are open to applying others. Clearly the combined effect of these two is synergistic, and technically they are compatible.

An activity which is synergistic to that of development for reuse is reengineering for reuse, enabling maximum benefit to be gained from preexisting code. REBOOT offers a method for finding potentially reusable parts in existing applications and can help re-engineer the code and package the embedded solutions and expertise in conformance with the REBOOT component model, to allow for future reuse

1.3.3 Storage and Dissemination of Components

The two SER technologies of most benefit in the activities of storing and disseminating reusable components and related information are REBOOT and EUROWARE, with some support also being provided by PROTEUS.

EUROWARE was developed as a follow on to REBOOT and allows reuse over wide areas, by utilising Internet techniques. It allows the utilisation over wide areas of reuse information, documents, and software components and modules. For larger organisations already using REBOOT clearly this enables reuse between sites and even continents, adding even further to the value of your organisation developing for and with reuse in a structured way. For smaller or less geographically diverse companies, there could be a longer term benefit of being able to trade software developed with REBOOT principles, or other suitable methodologies, with other organisations.

The EUROWARE toolset can also be used within a company intranet as an alternative to the REBOOT toolset, as it is simpler and can be used to introduce tool support quickly in an organisation which is in the process of introducing reuse.

REBOOT provides repository storage for reusable components, together with information about their reuse history. When it comes to the description of generic components (entire application frameworks or finer grain components) and the keeping of such components in a repository, there is some overlap between REBOOT and PROTEUS. However, since the technical solution is different (the REBOOT repository is represented as objects and relationships in an object oriented database, while the Proteus repository consists of PCL descriptions stored in ordinary files) the two can easily be combined. By storing PCL descriptions (at varying level of granularity) in the REBOOT repository benefit can be gained from the strong aspects of both technologies.

1.3.4   Development with Reuse

Development with reuse is the construction of new software with the help of reusable components. This includes the activities of:

- searching for a set of candidate components
- evaluating the set of retrieved candidate components to find the most suitable one
- if necessary, adapting the selected components to fit the specific requirements

The three main projects which support the activity of development with reuse are REBOOT, PROTEUS and EUROWARE. With the REBOOT methodologies already in place, there will already be software components stored for reuse purposes. The reusable components can be accessed either from a central repository or from external sources, such as the EUROWARE server, and the REBOOT tools enable these components to be evaluated. In addition to providing storage for reusable components, the EUROWARE server makes available other useful information for the purposes of development with reuse, such as information about training courses, helpful techniques for implementing development with reuse and so on.

The PROTEUS technology supports development with reuse, by providing the capability to store application frameworks and generic architectures. Together with the configuration management and version control features, PROTEUS allows easier generation of application instances, reusing core functionality between members of application families.

In addition to the three main projects which help in this area, EUROBANQUET focuses on evolution of banking software application to implement changes, due to legislation for example. It does not approach reuse per se. However, the project develops Reusable Banking Objects (RBOs), corresponding to real world objects, which are connected when building applications. REBOOT users in suitable industries could benefit by using Domain Analysis techniques for identifying suitable RBOs and then developing with reuse for banking and in similar industries such as insurance.

1.3.5 Evolution Control and Configuration Management

The main project which helps in the areas of configuration management and evolution control is PROTEUS, with EUROBANQUET providing configuration management capabilities for banking and similar applications. PROTEUS is strongly biased towards entire application frameworks, called system families. The project provides a means to handle the need for an application to evolve during its lifecycle in two directions: temporal evolution within a domain as the users requirements gradually change; and spatial evolution into parallel domains. The focus is on tracking the changes of the entire application framework and encouraging reuse at that level, without explicitly addressing the issue of reusing individual components. A framework idea, i.e. the idea of a generic entity explicitly constructed to be easily adaptable to changing requirements in a structured way, is applied in both PROTEUS and REBOOT. (Most individual components will also be constructed in this way in order to be truly reusable.) PROTEUS tools support versioning and configuring in a sophisticated manner, adding benefit to the REBOOT environment. PROTEUS tools also automate the processing necessary to produce the object code of a described system instance, a process which is not addressed in REBOOT.

For banking and similar applications, the EUROBANQUET Software Impact Analyser allows the detailed identification of propagation of a change throughout the code. However, there are no particular methods or approaches to managing the variants which result from the changes. The PROTEUS Configuration management tools could be used to control those changes.

1.3.6 Measurement of Product Quality

The REBOOT tools offer integrated metrics to measure quality of components. The notion of quality is based on a quality model that is customisable and that may take into account both language dependent and language independent metrics. A default model is provided for components written in C and C++.

1.4 The Typology of the SER Experiments

This section is meant to provide an overall view of the application of the different approaches represented in the consortium so as to define the boundaries of the experience gained within the SER project.

The wide variety of the domains addressed by the applications, the differences in the applied approaches, the range in scope and scale of the enacted programmes, make this book a useful source of tips and suggestions for future enactment of software evolution and reuse programmes in different scenarios.

Nonetheless, it is outside the purpose of this presentation to provide an exhaustive collection of application domains, scenarios and contexts. On the contrary, it should be regarded as a heterogeneous collection of experiences where it is likely that everybody could find useful hints, but where most likely nobody can find the exact picture of his/her reality. Every company, every department, and even every developer are unique and need to be addressed in details according to the specific needs. The rationale of the book is, nevertheless, that there exist general guidelines that were effective in the experience gained by the SER partners and that could trigger and help new experiments.

In order to better understand the specific context in which the experiments were carried out, a preliminary overview is provided where the different applications are analysed with respect to their main characteristics. In particular, the following ten attributes have been defined to characterise the applications represented within the SER project:

- **Pilot Company:** Identifies the company whose pilot project has been developed.
- **Consultant Company:** Identifies the coaching company, that is the company that provided the necessary methodological and technological support to carry out the experiment.
- **Size of involved team:**
  Regardless of the size of the Pilot company, the size of team/department involved in the application is reproduced in the table.
- **Domain:** Describes in one word the application domain of the pilot project.
- **Reuse experience:** Indicates the degree of previous reuse experience of the pilot company.
- **Size of application and Programming language:** Indicates the approximate size of the software application associated with the pilot project and the programming language used to develop it.
- **Type of software:** Indicates the type of software produced by the pilot projects: e.g. data-intensive applications, embedded systems, client/server applications, software intensive applications.
- **Scope:** Indicates whether the application impacted either a single product line or a larger domain. When referring to reuse experiments it indicates whether vertical (i.e. addressing a specific product area) or horizontal (i.e. aiming at producing general purpose components to be reused across an entire application domain) reuse were enacted.
- **Granularity:** Indicates the "size" of the reusable components being developed and reused. It may be fine-grained or coarse-grained or it may refer to object-oriented frameworks (O-O frameworks).
- **Technology:** The name of the ESPRIT project whose methodological and/or technological results were applied in the pilot experiment is provide.

The positioning of each application with respect to these attributes is reproduced in Table 1.1. and analysed in the following.

Table 1.1. shows that for all of the application experiments the *size* of the teams involved in the reuse and/or evolution projects is in the range of the tens regardless of the size of the organisation as a whole. This observation, together with the observed size of the applications involved in the experiments carried out within the

SER projects leads to the conclusion that the state-of-practice for the monitored sample of projects, as far as reuse enactment is concerned, is limited to small-scale-experiments. This is certainly due to the fact that most of the organisations are experiencing structured reuse for the first time or they only had limited experience and they chose to introduce it in the organisation in a step by step fashion (and rightly so).

Reports about "larger" experiments and programmes may be found in the literature but they are very limited in number. The investments, both in terms of resources and time, are at least one order of magnitude greater: they usually span over several years and involve at least one hundred people. These experiments are usually carried out by large companies (e.g. IBM, HP, Motorola) or governmental departments, especially in the United States. Relevant experiences from some such projects are presented in Chapter 2 as a complement to the experiences made by the SER partners.

As mentioned earlier and as shown by the table, the *application domains* addressed by the applications range over a number of different typologies: from avionics to banking, from telecommunication to manufacturing, from health care instruments to sound measurements. Similarly, the *type of produced software* goes from data-intensive applications to software intensive applications, from client server to embedded and to control systems.

The programming language used to implement the applications also varies: from Smalltalk to C++, from Ada to COBOL2, from C to COBOL.

The average *reuse experience* of the organisation is small to non existent with the only exception of one organisation that had a considerable amount of reuse experience prior to the development of the observed project and whose main purpose was to improve the reuse practice.

The *scope* of the experiments is equally distributed between horizontal and vertical reuse. In both cases the choice between vertical and horizontal scope is strongly influenced both by the company product strategy and by the opportunities available at the time of the experiment.

The *granularity* of the developed components is almost equally distributed between fine-grained (i.e. general purpose components) and coarse grained (i.e. entire applications or O-O frameworks).

Finally, all the experiments were carried out with the main goal of producing components for *internal reuse*.

The lack of uniformity in the application domain as well as in the type of produced software and in the programming language used in developing the applications certainly indicates that there does not exist any *a priori* bias against the enactment of a reuse-oriented approach and/or of an evolutionary approach. Each company has to make a choice based on pre-existing organisational, managerial and technical texture and after carefully evaluating the foreseen benefits against the prospect costs.

Table 1.1. Application Experiments Summary

	Pilot Company	Consultant Company	Size of Involved Team.	Application Domain	Previous Reuse experience
1	XiosBank	ATC & UMIST	medium	banking	none
2	Stentofon	SINTEF	20	intercom systems	some
3	Garex	SINTEF	30	communication systems	a lot
4	Bull	Bull		workflow support	some
5	SIA	TXT	8	avionics	some
6	IL	TXT	medium	health care instruments	small
7	BPM	TXT	25 (out of 130)	banking	small
8	Pirelli	TXT	20	manufacturing	small
9	Ericsson Radar	SINTEF	30	radar control	some
10	Norsonic	SINTEF	15	sound measurement instr.	none
11	Telecom Company	EP-Frameworks		telecom network mgmt	some
12	EP-Frameworks	EP-Frameworks	small	telecom gateway	small

Size of Application./ Language	Type of Software	Scope	Granularity	Technology
big applications/ Smalltalk	client/server system	horizontal	RBOs	EURO-BANQUET
300 KLOC/ C+SDL	embedded	productline / vertical	O-O framework	PROTEUS
500 KLOC/ C	embedded	productline / vertical	O-O framework	PROTEUS REBOOT
	Interactive sw tools	horizontal	large compo-nents	REBOOT
70 KLOC/ Ada	sw system	horizontal	fine grained	REBOOT
large applications/ C, C++	embedded	single prod-uct line	interpreters / O-O frameworks	REBOOT
100 KStatements / COBOL 2	data inten-sive systems	product-line	fine grained	REBOOT
/ C, C++	control sw systems	vertical	O-O framework	REBOOT
100 KStatements/ Ada, C++	embedded sw	horizontal	general components	REBOOT
100 KStatements/ C	embedded sw	vertical	O-O framework	REBOOT
50 KStatements	Data coll., pr., and rep.	vertical	O-O framework	REBOOT
108 KLOC	embedded	vertical	O-O framework	REBOOT

2 Benefits of Software Evolution and Reuse

Reuse is still not a common practice in many companies and this is certainly due to a complex combination of elements ranging from the lack of technical opportunities to the features of the domain at hand, from the business objectives of the companies to the characteristics and skills of the management, and so many more. Nevertheless, even when all the conditions for a reuse introduction program are in place, the problem that all companies considering the introduction of reuse have to face is to assess the economical and financial impact and the actual benefits of reuse in terms of time and costs savings, of improvement in the quality of the produced software and of increased productivity.

This chapter first presents the promises set forth by the proponents of software evolution and reuse. Then the experience gathered by those who have tried to realize the promised benefits in real projects is surveyed.

2.1 The Promises

According to Barry Boehm, software reuse is expected to be one of the major sources of costs savings in the software industry in the next few decades. Fig. 2.1., presented by Boehm at the STARS conference in 1991, illustrates the relative importance of the three major sources of expected savings in software development:

- working faster (due to better tools);
- working smarter (due to better processes for software development and better control over the processes by estimation, planning, assessment and improvement);
- work avoidance (due to increased reuse).

The baseline total is the expected expenditure without any improvement in software development technology.

This simple figure also demonstrates the general view of state-of-the-art companies and research communities: the focus is on reuse and process: tools are there to support improvements in the first two areas, and not as an end in themselves [KAR95].

This optimistic view about the benefits that reuse may yield, when introduced in a software producing organization, is reflected also by Capers Jones, author of many

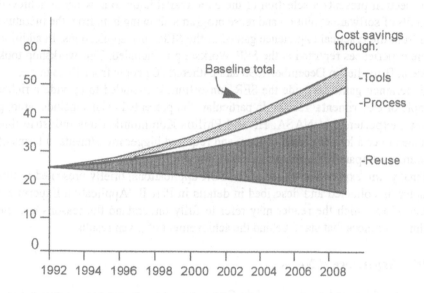

Fig. 2.1. Projected software development costs savings

articles and books about software quality and productivity and software development process improvement. In his [SPR94] he states that:

"Full software reusability programs tend to have the highest return on investment of any technology since software began (about $30.00 returned for every $1.00 invested)".

Such claims could be enough to convince managers of software producing organizations to undergo a reuse introduction and enactment program in their organizations, but what guarantees such a result? How can a manager be sure that such results will actually be achieved?

The expectations towards reuse have long been quite high and the promises quite alluring, but it isn't always possible to evaluate actual cost/benefits ratio when, again according to Capers Jones [SPR94],

"... costs are uncertain and can only be addressed with a high margin of error".

Managers are often faced with the choice between the promises their technical personnel presents them and the lack of an effective framework of reference to assess the actual reuse cost/benefit ratio in their own organizations up-front.

The literature, as a matter of fact, reports some success stories (unfortunately not so many failure stories are told) and an indication about the benefits of software evolution and reuse programs can be obtained analysing them.

2.2   What Has Been Delivered

This section presents a selection of the data available up to now about achieved benefits of software evolution and reuse programs, drawing both from the literature and from the practical experience gained in the SER pilot applications. In addition some experiences reported at the SER Workshop is included. This workshop took place in Bruxelles in December 1995 and gathered 80 people from 13 countries.

Experience gained outside the SER consortium is included to provide a richer sample of experimental results. In particular, the presented results include, among others, experience at NASA, HP and Philips Kommunikations Industrie that spanned over a longer period of time, and required bigger investments in terms of resources compared to the experiments monitored by SER.

Finally, the experience gained in the SER applications, briefly presented in this chapter, is collected and described in details in Part II "Application Experiment Reports" to which the reader may refer to fully understand the reasons and the technical choices that stand behind the achievement of given results.

2.2.1   Experience at NASA

At the NASA Goddard Space Flight Center a reuse program was carried out and monitored over a period of almost 10 years. Metrics were collected systematically over a long period of time in a relatively stable environment.

Data showing the trend in quality, cost and reuse from NASA/GSFC were presented by Frank McGarry at a seminar at the European Software Institute in October 1994 (see Fig. 2.2.)

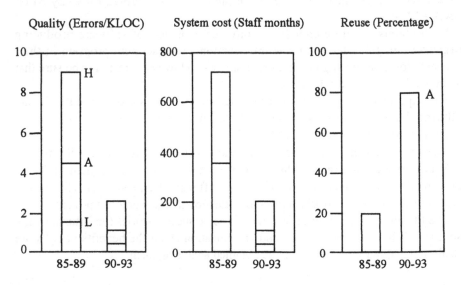

Fig. 2.2. NASA/GSFC quality, cost and reuse data

The figure shows that in the time span going from 1985 to 1989 the registered percentage of reuse was around 20% and the number of errors per KLOC was around 9. During the same period of time the cost for the development of a system in terms of effort was around 750 staff months.

In the years going from 1990 to 1993 it was possible to achieve an average reuse percentage of 80% and the quality of the produced software increased (i.e. the number of errors per KLOC dropped down to 2) whereas the productivity increased (i.e. the staff months necessary to develop systems of comparable size decreased to 210).

Overall, there was an improvement in quality (4 times) and productivity or cost (times) in connection with an increase in reuse. The data are collected from 7-8 similar systems in each time period. This does not provide any proof that reuse was the major contributor to these improvements, but other improvements, e.g. changes in tools (CASE) and process (Cleanroom), were introduced and measured in the same period, and neither gave more than limited improvements [KAR95].

2.2.2   Experience at HP

Metrics collected in two reuse programs at Hewlett-Packard also demonstrate improved quality, increased productivity, and reduced time to market. The results of economic cost-benefit analysis indicate reuse can provide a substantial return on investment [LIM94].

The first reuse program took place within the Manufacturing Productivity department of the HP's Software Technology Division which produces large-application software for manufacturing resource planning. The program started in 1993 and is ongoing.

The second program was initiated within the San Diego Technical Graphics Division, which develops, enhances and maintains firmware for plotters and printers. It started in 1987 and continues to the present.

The data collected was analysed and both quantitative and qualitative aspects of the reuse programs were estimated. As a part of this assessment, data on the improvement on quality, productivity and time-to market was analysed and documented as reproduced in Table 2.1.

Table 2.1. Effect of Reuse on Quality, Productivity, and Time-to-Market

Organisation	Manufacturing Productivity	**Technical Graphics**
Quality	51% defect reduction	24% defect reduction
Productivity	57% increase	40% increase
Time-to-market	Data not available	42% reduction

The conclusion drawn by the author for these products is that because software is reused multiple times, the defects fixes from each reuse accumulate, resulting in higher quality. Furthermore, reuse improves productivity by reducing the amount of time and labour needed to develop and maintain a software product.

Experience at HP has shown that the cost of creating reusable software varies depending on the type of software developed as presented in Table 4.

Table 2.2. Cost to produce reusable components and to reuse relative to traditional development

Domain	Air-traffic-control system	Menu- and forms-mgmt system	Graphics firmware
Cost to create reusable code	200%	120 to 480%	111%
Cost to reuse	10 to 20%	10 to 63%	19%

Finally, for these programs a profile has been produced presenting the economic return the organization receives for its efforts. This profile is presented in Table 2.3.

Table 2.3. Reuse program economic profiles

Organisation	Manufacturing Productivity	Technical Graphics
Time horizon	1983-1992 (10 years)	1987-1994 (8 years)
Start-up resources required	26 em[a]	107 em
Ongoing resources required	54 em	99 em
Gross cost	80 em	206 em
Gross savings	328 em	446 em
Return on investments (saving/cost)	410%	216%
Net present value	125 em	75 em
Break-even year (recoup start-up costs)	Second year	Sixth year

[a] em = engineering month

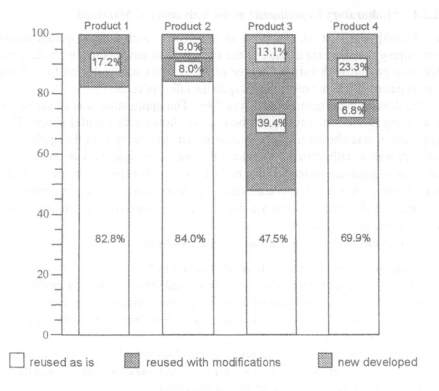

Fig. 2.3. Degree of Reuse of Application Software at Philips Kommunikations Industrie

2.2.3 Experience at Philips Kommunikations Industrie

At Philips Kommunikations Industrie - Nuremberg software reuse is seen as an excellent way for saving costs and development efforts [RAM96]. Four major products of the department for switching applications were evaluated: a digital switch, a container local exchange, a service switch from a different product family, a combined digital local and toll exchange similar to the first one.

The data was collected from products developed from 1991 through 1993 and it shows how the enactment of reuse led to a stable system architecture.

Reuse rates ranged between 60 and 80 percent with one exception were it did not reach 50 percent. The authors claim that this different result was partly due to the type of changes in the system requirements and partly to the fact that it belonged to a different product family. Adaptive reuse, that is, reuse occurred only after modifications, was in this case higher and the percentage of software that had to be written from scratch was well below 15%.

Design techniques especially tailored for the specific application domain and type of produced software were applied so as to maximise potential for reuse, but the cost associated with the introduction of this new technology is not provided by the authors.

2.2.4 "Laboratory Experiment" at the University of Maryland

In [Bas96], Basili et. al. report on an experiment with 8 development teams developing the same application in the same type of environment with the same technology, but with varying degree of reuse. Data was collected from these development efforts in order to investigate the effect of reuse.

The development environment was C++. The application was a system for managing home video rental, to be used by home video rental shops. This application was chosen in order to ensure that familiarity with the application domain was equally distributed among the teams. Several relevant libraries of reusable components were available to the teams, but the teams were free to make use of them or not. The teams consisted of students with reasonable experience in software development, and care was taken to ensure that overall capabilities of the teams were about the same.

The findings in this experiment are summarized below:

- Reuse rates ranged from close to zero% to close to 50%;
- High reuse projects (reuse rates between 40 and 50%) exhibited a productivity twice as high as that exhibited by the low reuse projects (reuse rates close to 0%);
- The error density observed in the high reuse projects was about 1/3rd of that observed in low reuse projects;
- Rework was much lower in high reuse projects than in the low reuse projects. This appeared to be primarily due to fewer errors. There was no statistically significant indication that errors were easier to find and repair.

2.2.5 Experience at Bull

As part of the REBOOT project, Bull conducted a pilot reuse program in a division producing software for client server based solutions in the office systems marketplace.

Initial analysis revealed a good potential for reuse in the division. This view was based on:

- the coexistence of several product streams and several sub-system development streams;
- recognition of the need to deal with a high rate of change in the operating and development systems;
- recognition of the immediate benefit of rationalizing the organizational structure to configure products from common sub-systems – thus releasing more resources to product improvement;
- recognition of the potential of the resulting organization to evolve a reusable component base to be used in product development.

Workflow systems were chosen as a pilot domain because this field is dependent upon, and builds on, many innovative and emerging technologies. The strategy was first to pilot the introduction of reuse to workflow systems development while involving the image and document processing teams. Then, the resulting reuse technology would be deployed to the entire department, and later, more generally within the company.

The overall benefits from this pilot program has been to position the company to offer more competitive products supplied in a shorter time. For example, the new version of the flowPATH product offers much more functionality which mostly comes from reuse of large components (e.g. ImageEditor, Communication layer, ContentPATH).

The additional costs has been outweighed by the benefits achieved during the program as is illustrated by the following concrete experiences:

- a sub-system, with a development cost of 4 PY (Person-Years), reused 5 times, saving 20 PY.
- a sub-system, with a development cost of 2 PY, reused twice, saving 4 PY.
- a framework, with a development cost of 2.5 PY, reused twice, saving 2 PY each time.
- a stand-alone product whose parts have been reused in another product, saving 0.5 PY.
- a generator, with a development cost of 2 PY, expected to save 4 PY.

The extra-cost for developing these reusable sub-systems and frameworks is about 30% of the normal development cost while costs of reuse are quite low (1-4 Person-Months) compared to the savings.

These benefits continue to grow as the number of projects reusing these well-designed and well-tested frameworks and sub-systems increases.

Last but not least, savings in maintenance are also substantial because the shared sub-systems are preserved as a single code base, thus keeping the support costs down to a fraction of what they would be if separate groups had to maintain their specific source code separately.

Other lessons learned in this committed and organised reuse program include:

- Reuse in-the-large (reuse of sub-systems) yields more benefits than reuse in-the-small.
- Development FOR reuse, coordinated with the development of application specific products, has had a beneficial impact on the architecture: it naturally leads to a clearer abstraction of the developed (sub)system that better supports late changes in requirements. Thus development FOR reuse adds to the quality of the developed application right from the start.
- Developing WITH reuse clearly motivates people to develop new reusable components.
- Market and return on investment must be carefully studied and followed-up. Since the technology is evolving rapidly, some components may become rapidly obsolete.

2.2.6 Experience at Ericsson Radar

Ericsson Radar is developing software for radar control systems for the military market. The company started to implement systematic reuse in 1993, following a feasibility study concluding that the domain was well suited for exploiting increased reuse, and outlining a reuse introduction programme inspired by the REBOOT methodology and based on the following main elements:

- establishment of an initial library based on parts of existing software;
- adaptation of the organization and development process for reuse;
- definition and collection of quality metrics for components and definition of a quality model for the library.

The development manager initiated the reuse introduction program and has also acted as *reuse board* and *reuse benefactor*. One developer assisted by one person form the SINTEF REBOOT team has acted as reuse *task force* and *reuse agent*[1].

At the end of the SER project, 4 applications have been completed. This has resulted in the development of 18 reusable components that have been used between 2 and 4 times (including the use in the project that developed the component). Two small components from earlier projects were reused in three projects.

The number of uses of each component varies between 2 and 4. Most of the components may be characterized as "global mechanism" components constituting a reusable software infrastructure for radar control applications and covering areas such as error handling, inter process communication, I/O processing, distribution management, graphic user interface and radar input simulation. There is also a bought in Ada library of standard algorithms and data types, registered as one component

A simple cost-benefit analysis of the reuse introduction program at ER is presented in Fig. 2.4. Already now the program has been profitable, with a net present value of 44 person months[2]. This is about 9% of the total effort on these projects, and about 15% of the total yearly software development effort of the company.

The extra cost for coordinated planning and follow up of projects is not included, but this is considered to be insignificant compared to the development costs.

These components, belonging mainly to a common infrastructure, are expected to be highly reusable in future applications. This is confirmed by the fact that the four applications taking part in this investigation span a wide range of different radar applications. 2 -3 reuses per year for the next years is a realistic assumption. One must expect some costs related to management and maintenance of the components,

---

[1] Reuse Initiator, Reuse Board, Reuse Benefactor, Reuse Task Force and Reuse Agent are important roles in a reuse introduction process as defined by the REBOOT methodology [Kar95]

[2] Assuming a rate of interest of 10%.

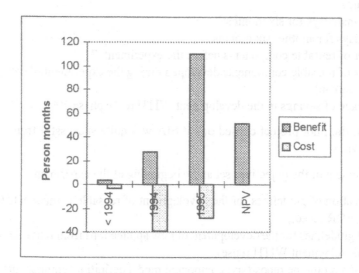

Fig. 2.4. Cost Benefit Analysis of Reuse Programme at Ericsson Radar

and this is estimated to 4 person months per year. A cost benefit analysis including estimated benefits for the next 3 years based on these assumptions, indicates a net present value after 6 years of 219 person months (for further details see Chapter 13).

2.2.7 Experience at SIA

Within the SER project, one of the experimentation with the REBOOT reuse methodology was carried out at SIA (Societa' Italiana Avionica) with the support of TXT Ingegneria Informatica.

The quantitative results of the pilot were quite encouraging. First of all the assessment of the company reuse maturity performed at the beginning of the project indicated that the company reuse strategy was overall an ad hoc procedure (level 1 of the REBOOT Reuse Maturity Model) mainly based on the capabilities and the skills of the single individuals even if the basis for a more structured way of working had been put.

At the end of the experiment, which lasted 18 months, the company had shifted to a more systematic reuse strategy; a higher level of commitment from the management was proved also by an increased allocation of resources, the number of people involved with the experiment grew from 2 to 8 during the experiment itself.

A set of guidelines had been produced and made available to the developers to support them in their activities (i.e. at level 2).

In addition to the data presented previously, the overall cost of the experiment, as well as the achieved savings, can be computed in terms of the following:

• Training of involved team: 5 days.

- Coaching:
  8 to 10 man days for six months;
  4 man days for another six months.
- Number of reusable components before the experiment: 7.
- Number of reusable components developed during the experiment (development FOR reuse): 40.
- Percentage of savings in the development WITH reuse phase 20%

Overall, the pilot project carried out at SIA was quite successful from several points of view:

1. Achievement of the objectives set at the beginning of the experiments:

- identification of guidelines for the development of reusable components (development FOR reuse);
- general guidelines for the development of new applications from reusable components (development WITH reuse);
- set up of a prototype repository, component model definition, components classification scheme definition.

2. Reuse culture dissemination within the organizations:

- training of development team members;
- involvement of selected development team members in the experiments;
- sensibilisation of management.

3. Identification of future areas of improvement.
4. Launch of corporate-wide programme for the realization of a census of the companies' assets. In particular, based on the pieces of component-related information that were identified and deemed significant within the pilot project a component profile has been defined to be filled in by the different departments in the companies of the corporate.
5. A new project was also launched which starting from EUROWARE technology is aimed at setting up a corporate wide repository for the classification, qualification, storage, search and retrieval of software assets.

For further details see Chapter 9.

2.2.8   Experience at Ericsson Software Technology

At the SER workshop in Brussels several case studies coached by Ericsson Software Technology were reported on.

In the telecommunication industry a company committed to an initial program of carefully managed and engineered reuse, which demonstrated the following benefits:

- developing one application along with a framework costs 1.4 times the cost of classical development;

- developing two applications along with a common reusable framework costs 1.75 times the cost of classical development;
- developing further applications using the framework reduces to 0.35 times the cost of development from scratch;
- by involving managers and engineers to plan and carefully engineer the reuse aspect of the work, casual reuse was eliminated - thus improving quality and reducing cost of repair activity.

2.2.9 Experience at SODALIA

Other experiences, in particular at SODALIA in Italy, were reported which demonstrate that this technology starts being applied successfully in industry.

From SODALIA, we learned that they have developed a series of small frameworks for Network Management and Data Collection & Analysis. New applications instantiated from the frameworks typically contain 20-30% of application-specific code meaning that the reuse rate achieved is 70-80%.

At organizational level, careful definition of the team in charge of developing frameworks is the key point: the team is set up with people coming from (and afterwards returning to) the team responsible for developing the applications by instantiating the frameworks so that creative work (designing frameworks) is not left to a unique/stable team. This also ensures that the design of the frameworks well takes into account requirements from the various future applications.

2.2.10 Experience with PROTEUS at Stentofon

Stentofon is an industrial company based in Trondheim, Norway. Their principal business is the production of customized internal intercom systems. They design and supply both the hardware and the software elements of these systems, and are a market leader in this area.

Stentofon has been in this business for many years, and has a significant share of the world market for this type of product. As a result, they have a large number of installations around the world - and many of these are different variants of the intercom product. Good hardware reliability also means that many older systems are still in use. In addition, it has always been - and continues to be - an important element of company strategy that Stentofon provides *customized* solutions for the special needs of individual customers. Combined with the large number of installations, this means that the company is responsible for the maintenance and further development of a very large variety of systems.

The large variety of systems produced by Stentofon, combined with the fact that new product development is always necessary to maintain a competitive edge, means that support for evolving systems is very important at Stentofon. Although evolution applies to both the hardware and software parts of the product, the issues discussed in this paper will be restricted to the software components.

The PROTEUS approach was applied at Stentofon, and the results obtained are evaluated and summarized in the following.

In particular, Table 2.4. shows the number of files, total number of lines of code, and number of versions per. file. Totally there were 721 manually maintained files and over 8000 versions of these. Note that all *generated* files (C files generated from SDL, Make dependency files, etc.) are omitted.

Table 2.4. Size Metrics for the Stentofon AICE Application

Type of source	No. of files	LOC	Versions pr. file
SDL	141	181421[a]	5-300
C	238	93500	10-100
Assembly	14	5266	10-100
Configuration files	11	918	5-50
ProgGen skeletons	288	3481	2-5
Foreign libraries	2		3-5
Makefiles, shell scripts	27	17224[b]	10-100

[a.] LOC for SDL source is approximated by the number of bytes in GR files divided by 30.
[b.] Five of the makefiles (14.263 LOC) are for recreation of old configurations.

Table 2.5. gives the size of the PCL model of the AICE application. The PCL model replaces the entries 'Makefiles/shell scripts' and possibly 'Configuration files' in Table 2.4., since when using the PROTEUS approach, they will be generated automatically from the PCL model.

Table 2.5. PCL model size data

Type of source	No. of files	LOC
Generic[a]	3	500
System specific[b]	7	1700

[a.] Common to all SDL-based systems in Stentofon
[b.] Of this ca. 75% was initially generated by ProgGen.

The evaluation has been based on three main criteria: (1) support for evolutionary development, (2) support for design-oriented development, and (3) flexibility of approach. Among the more advantageous experiences are:

- PCL allows a number of tasks to be done at higher abstraction level than before. Many highly inter-dependent details around the system and in the associated system building process are now automatically taken care of based on intentional specifications.

- Constructing a *total* system model covering all aspects of a system has been a favourable experience. Knowledge previously distributed and unavailable (person dependent) is now made visible and represented in a formal model. This information is also useful e.g. for internal communication and training. Modelling of system variability is however still somewhat incomplete.
- The choice of building the Repository on top of an existing version management system has been quite fortunate at Stentofon. Several years of evolution history are instantly available, presented in a graphical user interface.
- 'High' expressiveness of PCL is a vital factor for the success of PCL. It allows concise models, which are easy to understand and maintain as the system evolves. Intentional mechanisms are essential to handle the size and complexity of real systems.

Problem areas and deficiencies observed are:

- A crucial problem is to ensure consistency between the system model and the actual system. Structural and even some non-structural changes require that the system model is updated. More tight integration between the design tool and the PCL model is one possibility to alleviate this problem.
- A more practical obstacle in the experimentation has been the lack of availability, stability and maturity of the PCL toolset. The tools were originally released for a platform not available at Stentofon's development department.
- Fully automatic generation of run-time system configuration files has not yet been achieved.

This evaluation is based on the use of the SDL/88 version of SDL, which is the one currently in use at Stentofon. However, as tool support for SDL/92 is now becoming available, Stentofon will almost certainly start using SDL/92 in the near future. From a software engineering perspective, SDL/92 offers the following main advantages over SDL/88:

- it is easier to modularise, using *types* and *packages*
- variants can be described using *inheritance*
- it is possible to produce more generic descriptions, using *context parameters*

These improvements in the language make it easier to structure system descriptions, and to handle variability as systems evolve. However, these new language facilities do not seem to be sufficient to provide the support for evolution required in an industrial context. In fact, the use of inheritance can actually complicate management of the system descriptions through the extra dependencies that are introduced, and the wider range of translation strategies that become possible.

In conclusion, the expectation is that the use of SDL/92 will improve the software development process, but that the support provided by the ProgGen translation tool and the PCL toolset will, in total, be no less beneficial when using SDL/92 than when using SDL/88.

2.2.11 Experience with EUROWARE

Systematic reuse requires accurate analysis of organisation specific needs, long-term, top-down management support, implementation of reuse measurements, identification of expected key benefits, adequate technological support.

Once the necessary organizational, methodological and technical issues related to reuse have been defined and put in to practice, a complete reuse program also needs an appropriate automatic support, especially if the number of the reusable assets grows over the threshold of a few tens and/or if the organization is geographically distributed.

In fact, experience demonstrated that the following problems are among the major inhibiting causes

- difficulties in easily finding suitable software components
- difficulties in accessing software components
- lack of guarantee on the quality of the reusable components
- difficulties in accessing software components
- lack of comprehensive standards.

The EUROWARE project recognized these difficulties and provided a gradual path towards the setup of a unique, consistent, and practical repository for software reuse. The EUROWARE infrastructure is based on Internet and so targeted to a wide range of customers. Furthermore, it is open to the reusable assets: existing code, user interface elements, prebuilt components, developer's knowledge, experience, techniques, documentation, reports, forums.

EUROWARE was defined and developed having in mind several scenarios of use.

Among the others, it was thought as a Company Repository enabling transparent access to local and remote sites and making access and diffusion of the company assets easier thus maximizing reuse. As a side effect of the use of this company repository a uniform spread of a company culture would also be achieved.

The idea of a company repository appealed to a company that, after having experimented the REBOOT methodology achieved 20% costs reduction in the development of a pilot project.

The results of the experimental application also attracted to the management attention and convinced them of the validity of a reuse introduction program on a larger scale.The top management therefore committed to support further effort to spread the reuse culture and to enact reuse across the company.

A few weaknesses were though detected in the overall company process that could hinder reuse on a larger scale, namely:

- slow circulation of the information;
- cumbersome maintenance of the reusable assets repository (initially maintained in paper form and then changed into a prototype automatic local repository)
- time consuming browsing of the repository due to the lack of attention devoted to the presentation aspects of the prototype repository;

- difficulties in collecting feed-back from reusers;
- difficulties in tracking the complete reuse history.

The possibility to overcome these problems using the EUROWARE infrastructure was evaluated and deemed appropriate. This approach also takes into account the possibility to further increase savings thanks to an increase in the number of reusable components and the possibility to make them available through a distributed, company-wide repository.

A further pilot project has been launched which is currently in progress.Final data are not yet available, but the initial evaluation based on which the company invested in this larger-scale experiment led to the definition of the following goals:

- reduction of the time spent in circulating new reusable components (75%)
- increase of frequency of classification, storage, search and retrieval
- reduction of time spent in carrying out these activities (30%)
- increase in the number of successful classification, storage, search and retrieval

2.3 Summing Up

The presented data fall in two groups; data on costs and achieved savings, and data on the effect of increased reuse on productivity, time-to-market and quality.

Data in the first group, costs and achieved savings, is summarised in Table 2.6. In addition to data from the projects presented above, we have also included data from the US Federal Aviation Administration's Advanced Automation Systems project reported in [Mar91] (labelled Air Traffic Control in the table), and from a menu and forms management system written in Ada reported in [Fav90] (labelled Ada Menu and Forms in the table)

The most obvious observation to make from these data is probably that there is a lot of variation:

- The return on investment for the observed reuse effort ranges from 180% to more than 400%. However it is worthwhile to note that the highest return on investment was observed in the project that lasted the longest.The break-even point ranges from 2 to 6 years. However, around 2-3 years seem to be more common than 6 years.

- The cost to develop reusable components ranges from 10% extra to several hundred percent extra compared to the cost of developing the same component without considering reuse..

- The cost to integrate a reusable component compared to the cost of developing the needed functionality from scratch ranges from 5% to 60%.

The data in the other group, the effect of increased reuse on productivity, time-to-market and quality summarized in Table 2.7. also show considerable variation. However it appears that there is a clear correlation between reuse rate and both productivity and error rate. Increasing the reuse rate from close to zero to close to

Table 2.6. Summary of Reuse cost data

Source	Period of observation (years)	Return on investment (%)	Break-even year	Cost to dev. RCs (%)	Cost to reuse (%)
HP Man. Prod.	83-92	410	2nd		
HP Technical Graphics	87-94	216	6th	111	19
Air Traffic Control				200	10 to 20
Ada Menu and Forms				120 to 480	10 to 63
Bull Workflow	91-94			130	5 to 10
Ericsson Radar	93 - 95	180	2nd	110-130	5 - 25
Ericsson Telecom			2nd	140	35

50%, a 50% increase in productivity and halving of the error rate will not be unusual. For the time-to-market we only have data from one programme, showing a decrease of about 40%.

There are two factors that may explain the variation in achievements between the different projects.

Firstly these results have been obtained in different contexts: in different application domains, in different markets, using different development environments, and applying different reuse approaches. In the following chapter we try to relate the experiences to a few typical scenarios which we hope will help identifying the experiences most relevant for a reader planning a new reuse programme in a particular context. For now we conclude that there is considerable experimental evidence that SER is a viable approach to significant improvements in software engineering effectiveness.

Secondly there is the inherent difficulty in measuring the achievements in software projects and the lack of standardised metrics. For instance the numbers reproduced here have been produced in several different ways:

- In HP Manufacturing Productivity and HP Technical Graphics one compares the productivity and error rate in the entire products (including reused parts) with the productivity and error rate in the parts that were developed new.
- In NASA and the other HP firmware division one compares the productivity and reuse rate at the beginning and end of a period where a significant increase in reuse rate has been achieved, but where also other improvements is likely to have had an effect.
- In the laboratory experiment at Maryland University one compares the results achieved by different teams developing similar applications with different reuse rates.

It seems likely that the remarkably good results in NASA and the HP firmware division is due to the influence of other improvements in addition to reuse.

Table 2.7. Summary of data on effect of reuse on productivity, time-to-market and quality

	Reuse rate before (%)	Reuse rate after (%)	Product-ivity increase (%)	Time-to-market reduction (%)	Reduction in error rate
NASA	20	80	300[a]		70
HP Man. Prod.	0	68	57		51
HP Technical Graphics	0	32	40	42	24
Other HP firmware div.	5	80	400		
Lab. exp. at Maryland Univ.	0-10	40-50	225		65

[a.] Derived from system cost, assuming that the system size has been stable in the period of observation

3 Lessons Learned

As discussed in the previous section, there are many issues that direct the design of an appropriate evolution and reuse program in a given organisation, and each organisation has to find a solution suited for its particular situation. Nevertheless it is possible to define a few typical scenarios that will be close to the actual situation in many companies.

In this section three such typical scenarios are identified and presented along with relevant experience and advice based on the SER experiments. The idea is that the reader will find a scenario which is close to the situation of his company and benefit from the lessons learned by companies in a similar situation.

These scenarios are:

- *Scenario 1 - Product Family,* applicable to organisations who typically develops applications in an ad-hoc manner, with similar applications often being developed independently, either from scratch or by slightly tailoring an applications which is known to already exist, and focusing on reconciling disparate applications and optimising commonality to achieve a coherent product family with a core of reusable assets.
- *Scenario 2 - Component Based Application Development,* applicable to organisations needing to develop very different applications while still wanting to exploit the benefits of reuse, and focusing on the development and acquisition of reusable components to facilitate the future development of diverse new applications.
- *Scenario 3 - Application Framework,* focusing on the design, development and management of a generic application framework and associated product family, and applicable to organisations delivering many similar but still significantly different applications.

The chosen grouping aims at presenting the strategy adopted in carrying out SER applications. The experience gained is summarised and factors out the common traits of similar experiences among those monitored within the SER project. This approach chosen in presenting the lesson learned is meant to enable the reader to identify among the "guidelines" presented in this section the ones that are most relevant to her/him.

Domain-dependent solutions and strategies adopted in specific applications shall also be emphasised.

3.1   Scenario 1 - Product Family

Product development is often undertaken on an ad-hoc basis, without any serious attempt to exploit commonalities between applications, although significant overlaps in requirements between applications in the same domain usually exist. Ad hoc reuse of parts from existing applications may happen, even reuse of an entire application by adapting it to satisfy a slightly different set of requirements, but without any formal recording of the commonalities. This results in disparate applications, with no formal knowledge about commonalities, and no common maintenance and evolution of parts of the same origin.

Each of these applications does in fact form part of an informal application family, and could have been created from one architectural framework, with a set of reusable components providing the tailoring for specific customers, platforms etc.

When this second approach is taken, it offers huge benefits in terms of:

- reduced development cost, owing to the fact that development work which has already been carried out elsewhere will not be repeated
- reduced development time, because there is less to do
- better quality, because new applications is built from proven parts
- consistency of applications' content and their 'look-and-feel', because they share the same components

Object oriented languages have proven to be well suited to implement such application frameworks, and the term O-O Framework is one if the hottest buzz words of software engineering today. On the other hand there are also many examples of successful application frameworks implemented in other languages.

In this section we focus on the influence of the existing disparate applications, leaving more general issues concerning the management and exploitation of a framework to scenario 3.

3.1.1   The Experiments

Several SER applications match this scenario and confirm the benefits listed above.

In the Ericsson Telecom case the product is a set of applications for the management of telecommunication networks. Originally disparate sets of applications existed for the main markets, in order to comply with local standards. The sets shared some reusable components for communication with the network, but this constituted only a small part of each application.

In order to reduce time to market and improve quality, it was decided to base future development on the O-O Framework approach. The objective is to develop one framework for each type of application, and instantiate it to comply with the standards of each main market.

So far a framework for one type of application has been developed and it has been instantiated for two markets. Instantiation for a third market and the development of two new Frameworks is under way.

In the Norsonic case (see Chapter 14) the application domain is sound measurement instruments. The company had a range of instrument models varying in size, performance and flexibility to cover diverse applications of such instruments. Despite a lot of overlapping functionality between the instruments, the software had mostly been developed from scratch in each case, with only occasional copy-and-past reuse of small code fragments.

To meet a need for rapid development of customised models for niche markets, the company had decided to base future software development on the framework approach.

A framework is now being designed. The plan is to launch the first instrument with software based on the framework by the end of next year, that is 2 years after the start of the reuse initiative.

3.1.2 Lessons Learned

Cost/benefit: Relative cost data from Ericsson Telecom are presented in Fig. 3.1. As can be seen, when including the cost of developing the framework, the cost of developing the first application with the framework is about 50% higher than the typical cost of developing an application before the framework was introduced. However, as the cost of instantiating the framework is only 36% of the cost of developing applications the traditional way, this extra cost is recouped already after the second instantiation. This means a quick return on investment and low risk, at least for moderate size frameworks.

Domain Analysis: In Norsonic the Proteus domain analysis method [Pro93] was used to analyse and model the requirements in the domain in order to identify what is stable and what is varying and to assess the applicability of the framework ap-

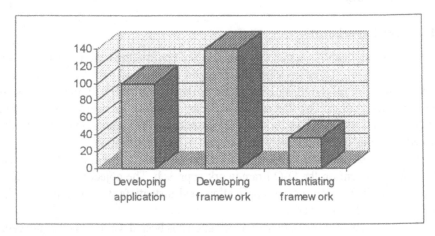

Fig. 3.1. Relative Development Costs at Ericsson Telecom

proach to the domain. The analysis of existing applications provided major input to this analysis.

The analysis convinced the company that the framework approach would fulfil their needs. Also the models that were produced proved useful as a means to conciliate the views of different product teams.

In Ericsson they did not put so much emphasis on domain analysis, but proceeded more directly to framework design using the Group Dynamic Technique [KAR95]. This technique relies on the cooperation of representatives from the different markets and from different parts of the organisation in the design process to ensure identification of commonalities and domain coverage.

How Much of Existing Disparate Applications can be Reused in a Framework?
In both cases the idea has been to reuse as much as possible of the existing disparate applications when building the framework. In the Ericsson Telecom case, parts adapted from the existing applications constitute about 50% of the framework. However encouraging the results may sound, the overall experience was not so good. Generally, the reused parts required significant changes to be made usable in the framework, more than 20% on the average, and testing required more time than normal. Unfortunately this was not actually measured, but is based on the subjective judgement of the developers, who also believe that it would have been less work to develop these parts from scratch.

In Norsonic one also expects that close to 50% of the framework can be built by adapting parts from existing applications, but in reality the emerging framework design differs in many respects from the existing applications. The reason is that when designing a framework, localising the impact of variability is a major concern that often leads to other structures than what is natural when designing isolated applications.

In conclusion there is reason to be critical about the reusability of the code of existing applications for building a framework, and not too many benefits may be expected from such reuse. Fortunately this does not compromise the profitability of the framework approach.

Organisational Issues: Often the organisation and the development process that produced the disparate applications will not be suitable for exploiting and evolving a framework. Otherwise, why was not a framework built in the first place?

Norsonic had a purely project oriented organisation where each development of a new instrument was an autonomous project with no incentive to cooperate and coordinate with other projects. This was conceived as a major obstacle to exploiting reuse. Therefore the first step was to change the organisation. Now there is one team responsible for each major subsystem of the framework. Each team both develops the common parts of their subsystem and adapts it for the development projects. The development projects contract these teams to develop the subsystems they need for their product.

To ensure that subsystem teams have sufficient knowledge of current and future market needs, so called specifications groups has been organised for each main market. A specification group consists of marketing people working in the market segment and representatives for the subsystem groups. The responsibility of the market groups is to keep domain models up to date and specify new instruments.

A similar approach is taken in Ericsson Telecom. Originally there were independent teams for each market with little cooperation between them. After the experiment the teams remained but their responsibilities changed. In addition to being responsible for delivering applications to its market, each team will now also be responsible for one or more frameworks and for assisting the other teams in instantiating the framework for their markets.

To ensure good contact between the team responsible for a framework and the respective markets, reference groups have been organised. A reference group consists of representatives of the team responsible for a framework and for the users of the framework, and is responsible for coordinating the evolution of the framework.

In general we believe that the adoption of the framework approach requires changes to the organisation in line with the solutions adopted at Ericsson Telecom and Norsonic, in order to control the future exploitation and evolution of the framework.

3.2   Scenario 2 - Component Based Application Development

Once organisations are aware of the benefits of adopting a reuse culture and have decided to follow this path, it is necessary to find the appropriate underlying technology to support software reuse and enable the maximum benefit to be gained. Aspects which need to be covered are:

- populating the reuse repository - developing, extracting and importing components
- classifying and storing components for maximum efficiency of retrieval and access
- using the repository components when developing applications

3.2.1   The Experiments

The development, extraction and import of component in order to populate an organisation's repository are activities that require special care; in fact the success of a reuse program relies, among the other factors, upon the quality and reusability of the components that are made available to the developers.

This approach to reuse was adopted at SIA (see Chapter 9) where the pilot project led to the definition of a set of guidelines specially suited for Ada applications in the avionics domain. After reaching the end of the pilot project, the management decided to launch an inventory for all the software developed not only by SIA, but by the entire corporate (a large Italian aerospace company). The purpose of the inventory is that of classifying, according to a standard form, all the existent software and to identify areas with high potential for reuse. The effort for developing components FOR reuse will then be focused in these areas making use of the guidelines defined during the pilot experiment.

The problem of specialising methodologies and techniques in a particular application domain is not unique to high technology companies such as aerospace ones may be. As a matter of fact, the SER consortium monitored a similar experience, given the due differences, in the banking domain. At Banca Popolare di Milano (for further details see Chapter 11), as it is very common in the banking domain, software applications are data-intensive. Furthermore, the development team uses a tool for the automatic generation of code starting from the description of the data structures handled by the applications. Thus, interesting reusable assets are represented by the data descriptions maintained within the tool and, in order to define reusable structures, the emphasis of the pilot was on domain analysis.

The same way there are similar experiences in different domains, there are also different experiences in similar domains. The approach adopted at Xios Bank (for further details see Chapter 5), in fact, is centred around the definition and development of building blocks, the so called Reusable Banking Objects (RBOs), that enable to rapidly developing banking applications maintaining a coherent interface with the bank user. According to this approach, the developer of a new application will not so much be concerned with issues such as business rules, data storage, retrieval, presentation, etc.; these will be provided by the RBOs themselves. The developer will be able to build a new application visually interconnecting RBOs using events and messages provided by a workbench.

The solution adopted, at Ericsson Radar (for further details see Chapter 13) was a step by step program for:

- establishing an initial library based on portions of existing software;
- documenting the process according to a company standard;
- re-engineering and packaging existing components.

In order to foster reuse though, a substantial organisation re-structuring was performed and metrics for evaluating the benefits and costs of reuse were defined and data was collected.

3.2.2 Lessons Learned

Setting up a repository is not enough to ensure that actually reusable components are stored and are actually reused. First of all, special care must be devoted to the definition of an appropriate component model so as to identify all useful information (e.g. specification, design, code, tests, documentation) which can be reused as well as the characteristics which will help in the selection when reusers will browse the repository in search of the components they need. Secondly, the repository must be easily accessible and well supported (e.g. the web greatly facilitates access to a centralized catalogue). Finally an appropriate classification schema must be defined. That is not an easy task. Such a classification schema can only be obtained by a rigorous analysis of the domain while refinements will undoubtedly be required afterwards.

3.3   Scenario 3 - Application Framework

In order to prevent product development occurring on an ad-hoc basis, and to increase quality of developed applications, an architecture framework can be designed, in order to be able to use this and a repository of reusable components to produce and manage application families. This scenario contains many of the same processes as in Scenario 2, although because the starting point is from nothing rather than from a set of disparate applications, it is easier to develop a stronger, better managed architecture framework, repository and application family.

3.3.1   The Experiments

The experiments that are most relevant to this scenario are Telecom Gateway, IL, Pirelli and GAREX, but experiences from the Ericsson Telecom and Norsonic frameworks discussed in scenario 2 will also be included where appropriate.

In Telecom Gateway the application domain is a system for collecting administrative data from the various network elements of a communication network and distributing them to various administrative applications for further processing and reporting. The framework has been built and instantiated four times over a period of two years. It is now the basis of a very profitable product line of the company.

GAREX is a company that delivers voice communication systems for traffic management. The company has delivered customised solutions based on a common generic framework to many international airports and harbours over a period of more than 10 years. After being extended and instantiated many times the GAREX framework has become rather complex and although it is flexible enough to allow many deliveries to be built without writing new code, the benefits of reuse is to some extent compromised by the complexity of configuring the framework for a particular set of requirements. To overcome such problems GAREX has experimented both with REBOOT and Proteus technology.

Instrumentation Laboratory is a company that builds critical health-care instruments (blood analysis and electrolyte). The type of applications developed by IL is represented by complex medical machines corresponding to complex software systems and embedded applications. In order to enact reuse within the company, IL software applications are developed following a particular layered architecture consisting of:

- hardware platform;
- firmware;
- intermediate layer 1: interpreters of high level languages for the definition of abstract machines;

- intermediate layer 2: interpreters between basic arithmetic libraries and the interface with the operator of the medical device.

The structure of the interpreters is such that they can often be reused in different contexts (i.e. for the development of applications for different devices of the same line)

Pirelli is a company with a number of large factories worldwide. It is structured into two sectors: Tyre and Cables. As far as the Tyre sector is concerned, there exist 11 plants located in Europe. All the plants develop similar, but not identical, products and make use of similar, but not identical, manufacturing equipment.

The usual life-cycle of an application encompasses several steps as reproduced in the following:

- development of a system for a pilot site but with requirements generalised through international working groups;
- operation of the system at the pilot site and new release of the system based on the feedback obtained from its operation;
- customisation of the system for a number of other sites.

The customisation process is not in general a trivial one due to the differences among different plants:

- product related differences due to requirements on product characteristics
- manufacturing equipment differences;
- environmental differences mainly due to the specific way of working and the manufacturing process of each single site;
- cultural differences due to the different technical background of the operators;
- linguistic differences due to the location of the plants.

In this scenario, it was possible to achieve up to 50% of reuse in the implementation of the manufacturing scheduling applications. In particular, the architecture of the system was defined in such a way that the manufacturing process and the production orders as well as the database, the HCI and the scheduling algorithm could be reused almost entirely from one application to the other.

3.3.2 Lessons Learned

Cost / Benefits: Unfortunately sufficient quantitative results to present a cost benefit analysis for these applications has not been made available to date, but all companies claim that their frameworks are very profitable. In all cases qualitative results have been largely recognised and the major benefits are the increased flexibility and reduced time-to-market, making it possible to rapidly develop applications satisfying the requirements of particular customers or market niches.

Representation of the Framework Architecture: The Telecom Gateway and Ericsson Telecom frameworks are written in C++ and the architectures are represented as a set of cooperating classes, many of them abstract classes.

The GAREX framework is written in C but has a design inspired by O-O principles. Here the lack of a formal model at the architecture level is felt as a serious problem, but then one must keep in mind that this framework is both 10 times as big and almost 10 times as old as the other two.

In search of a solution to this problem, an experiment with using PCL (Proteus Configuration Language) to describe the architecture of a part of the GAREX framework has been carried out by SINTEF DELAB (see Chapter 7). PCL proved to be very well suited to this kind of modelling and the conclusion was that a PCL model of the framework would be very useful.

Distinguishing Common and Varying Parts: In the C++ frameworks the primary mechanism used to express the distinction between the common and varying parts is inheritance. The common properties of objects are expressed as abstract classes which are specialised in the instantiations of the framework. In some cases more complex schemes are needed and for these cases some of the design patterns published in [Gam94] has proved very useful.

In the GAREX framework the primary mechanism is branching on configuration variables and replacement of entire components. This is powerful and allows for fine grained configuration of properties at instantiation time, but has the drawback that instantiation becomes complex.

The experiment with PCL mentioned above also included the exploitation of PCL facilities to model variability. It seems that by exploiting the attribute mechanism of PCL one would be able to hide many of the low level details plaguing configuration today and facilitate instantiation of the framework at a higher level of abstraction, and that this would yield very high benefits. Unfortunately the Proteus tools are not yet available on commercial terms and GAREX is therefore reluctant to take them into use.

In the case of the IL application some of the reusable components are actually interpreters of special domain specific high level languages, facilitating the description of the customisation of the component at a problem oriented level.

In conclusion it seems clear that object oriented design notations and programming languages have an advantage in describing customisable components due to their support of inheritance, but there are also many other useful techniques equally well supported by other languages. The important thing is to have an abstract model of the variability of the domain and an implementation that allows instantiation at that level, without having to care about all details.

The Effect of Aging: With young frameworks that have been instantiated only a few times, instantiation is normally smooth. The design is clean and well understood, the opportunities for customisation are well structured and well documented and the number of customised components available for reuse is small. Both the Telecom Gateway and the Ericsson Telecom case report this experience.

But how is the situation when the framework has been instantiated hundreds of times over many years as in the GAREX case?

In GAREX it is often possible to satisfy a new customer without any new development, just by instantiating the framework with existing parts. But this has become an increasingly complex, error prone and costly task. To counteract this development the company has decided on a number of measures:

- Change the organisation from project oriented to framework oriented to better control the complexity of the framework.
- Reuse of partially configured subsystems to achieve reuse at a coarser granularity
- Reuse of requirements specification components with associated directions for how to instantiate to achieve the corresponding functionality.

The lesson here is that although one expects a stable domain to ensure long lifetime for the framework and high benefits, one must be aware of the effect of aging and take measures to control the growth of complexity.

4 Conclusions and Recommendations

The purpose of this chapter is to summarise the experience that has been presented in the previous chapters and to identify the directions and trends that may be useful for the planning and follow up of similar software evolution and reuse enactment programmes in other companies. In particular, possible relationships among the observed results have been highlighted.

A quite evident relationship is represented by the reuse rates achieved by the projects examined in this book. The percentage of reuse achieved seems to be strictly related with the characteristics of the application domain: a different trend is usually observed for single-product vs. multi-product (i.e. homogeneous vs. heterogeneous) domains as well as for stable vs. unstable domains. That is to say, the possibility of reusing is higher for organisations working in a narrow market sector where there exists a certain homogeneity among the developed products or for company departments dealing with specific product lines as compared to the rates achievable by companies operating in a diverse market sector. Of course it is also important to take into account the relative size of the company/department and the number of product lines in the same market sector.

The achieved reuse rate also varies with the type of reusable artefact as discussed in section 4.1.

General methodological conclusions can be drawn also by observing the results achieved when reusable components were developed starting from existing software versus the results achieved when they were developed from scratch as pointed out in section 4.2.

Finally, general observations on the benefits which may be expected from the enactment of an evolution and reuse approach as well as the associated costs and savings, are discussed in sections 4.3 and 4.4 respectively.

Far from being based on a thorough statistical analysis of a complete sample of cases, the following express the educated interpretation by the authors of the available material on experience with software evolution and reuse up till now.

4.1   Reuse Rates

4.1.1   General Component Reuse

Reusing general infrastructure components is probably the most easy and low risk way to get started with an SER oriented software development practice. This category encompasses such things as graphical user interfaces, persistent data storage and retrieval, exception handling, concurrency, distribution, and communication among others.

Reusing such components only, does not normally lead to very high reuse rates; 20 to 30% seems to be achievable, depending on the complexity of the application. On the other hand, the extra costs to make such components reusable is generally low and they tend to be profitable after one or two reuses. Often acceptable components in this category may also be bought in at a reasonable price. Therefore reuse enactment programmes based on this approach normally require low initial investments and break even already after a few years. Values around 2-3 years has been observed. Furthermore such components tend to be highly reusable, since they implement requirements common both within and between application domains. This means that good return on investment can be expected. For instance in the Ericsson Radar case the expected return on investment if we include anticipated reuse of the existing components for the next 3 years is around 500%.

Also in this case however, such results do not come for free. It is necessary to provide appropriate incentives and adapt the organisation and work processes appropriately.

4.1.2   Domain Specific Reuse

Extending the scope to reuse of domain specific components is more challenging. Good domain knowledge and skilled designers are required to identify the right components that will be useful in different applications in the domain, and an appropriate infrastructure supporting the configuration of applications from standard components in a flexible way will normally be needed.

The risk is often higher than in the case of general components, but this depends on how well understood the domain is.

The reward is higher reuse rates and the benefits that follows: higher productivity, shorter time-to-market and better quality. For instance in the "laboratory experiment" at Maryland University, where both general purpose and domain specific components were made available to the development teams, the best teams achieved reuse rates close to 50%, and productivity and error rate scores that were more than 100% better than those achieved by the teams not exploiting reuse.

The Eurobanquet experiment (Chapter 5) is also an example of this kind of approach, but based on the relatively novel paradigm of reusable business objects, which can be seen as the latest advancement in the understanding of how to construct domain specific components. Unfortunately we do not have data on achieved reuse rates.

4.1.3   Application Frameworks

Application frameworks normally give even higher reuse rates. Around 80% has been observed in several cases. However this approach requires that the application domain is well understood and exhibits sufficient stability that the development and repeated instantiation of a framework is feasible. Examples among the SER experiments of domains where this approach has been successfully applied is airport communication systems (GAREX), telecommunication network management (Ericsson Telecom) and noise measurement (Norsonic).

The up-front investment is higher with the framework approach compared to the component oriented approaches, because the entire framework has to be developed before there are any savings. On the other hand the savings are also high, and according to our observations a framework is typically profitable already after the 2nd or 3rd instantiation.

4.2   Reengineering Existing Software vs. Building from Scratch

Existing applications are definitely valuable sources of domain knowledge in the process of identifying and developing reusable components in a domain. This is stressed by domain analysis methods and also confirmed by the SER experiments.

To which extent it is wise to actually reuse and adapt parts of existing applications when building reusable components or frameworks is more doubtful. Unfortunately we don't have any data about this, but the feeling among people that have tried is that this is a tedious and error prone work, and that developing the component from scratch may be more efficient.

It appears that general purpose components are easier to extract than domain specific components, probably because general purpose functionality is more easily recognisable and tend to be needed several places in an application and therefore more likely to be isolated in components already than is the case with domain specific functionality.

4.3   Expected Benefits

As already pointed out in Chapter 2, there are sufficient quantitative results on the positive effect of reuse on productivity and error rate to be fairly confident that there is such an effect. The size of the effect varies considerably between observations, so it is hard to give any formula, but doubling productivity and halving error rate seem to be realistic goals for a reuse enactment program starting from a baseline with little reuse at all.

For the effect of reuse on time-to-market, we have one observation from HP Technical Graphics reporting a 42% reduction, resulting from a 6 year programme achieving a reuse rate of 32%. However the corresponding baseline reuse rate is not given.

4.4   Costs and Savings

There is normally some extra costs associated with the development of reusable components compared to implementing the corresponding functionality considering the need of one application only. Experience range from 10% extra to several 100% extra. However most observations are in the low end of this range and the savings by reusing the components easily outweighs these costs, leading to good returns on investment. Values from 200% and up has been observed.

The lead-time to breaking-even depends on the type of approach, the complexity of the domain.and size of application.

Starting modestly with general purpose components normally breaks even after a few years.

4.5   Conclusion

Above we have tried to identify trends and patterns in the material we have analysed, and this will hopefully be of some help in connection with the launch of similar improvement programs. Still an obvious conclusion is that experiences are diverse and costs and benefits hard to predict.

A possible solution to tackle the uncertainty related to the introduction of a new technological approach such as software reuse or evolution is that of launching limited scale programmes on a set of pilot applications rather than initiating a full scale reuse enactment programme. Such a solution is often chosen above all others by the managerial staff of medium size enterprises as well as large enterprises. Project are then monitored so as to determine the weaknesses in the enactment process and to identify possible areas for improvement before the introduction is enlarged to the whole company. At the same time cost saving trends are identified and the basis for a projection about future expectations is established.

This incremental approach to reuse introduction is very sensible and usually recommended, but as far as the objective data that can be obtained from the pilots one should always remember that they are usually only partial results.
In other words, real savings may be obtained only in the long term and there is no quick *silver bullet* that can lead to fully appreciate the benefits of software evolution and reuse programs for minimal costs, and create order of magnitude improvements in less than three to four years.

The investments in the reuse introduction program in terms of incentives, organisational restructuring and personnel training, as well as resource allocation, highly influences the results of the program itself. Similarly, strong commitment on the management side is essential to overcome the break even threshold.

As far as the influence of a methodology rather than another is concerned, it is reasonable to assume that any of the presented approaches could work as long as it takes into account the entire range of aspects that make a software producing company work: organisational, managerial, methodological as well as technical and technological.

Part II
Application Experiment Reports

Part II includes, for each application monitored within the SER project, a short description of the main characteristics, a more detailed description of the specific context the application was developed in, and a description of the main results and lesson learned.

The material reproduced here is partially the product of application experiments that have been carried out outside the SER project and that have kindly agreed to share their results with the consortium.

For each application the following characteristics are reproduced:

- **Pilot Company**:
  Identifies the company whose pilot project has been developed.
- **Consultant Company:**
  Identifies the coaching company, that is the company that provided the necessary methodological and technological support to carry out the experiment.
- **Size of involved team:**
  Regardless of the size of the Pilot company, the size of team/department involved in the application is reproduced in the table
- **Domain:**
  Describes in one word the application domain of the pilot project
- **Reuse experience:**
  Indicates whether the pilot company had previous reuse experience or not. In case there had been previous experiences with reuse it is specified whether they were small or more significant both in terms of time span and size.
- **Size of application and Programming language:**
  Indicates the approximate size of the software application associated with the pilot project an the programming language used to develop it.
- **Type of software:**
  Indicates the type of software produced by the pilot projects, for instsnce data-intensive applications, embedded systems, client/server applications, software intensive applications

- **Scope:**
  Indicates whether the application impacted either a single product line or a larger domain. When referring to reuse experiments it indicates whether vertical (i.e. addressing a specific product area) or horizontal (i.e. aiming at producing general purpose components to be reused across an entire application domain) reuse were enacted.
- **Granularity:**
  Indicates the "size" of the reusable components being developed and reused. It may be fine-grained or coarse-grained or it may refer to object-oriented frameworks (O-O frameworks).
- **Technology:**
  The name of the ESPRIT project whose methodological and/or technological results were applied in the pilot experiment is provided.

As far as the detailed description is concerned, the focus is on a description of the application domain, the motivation that led the company to adopt reuse, previous experiences and existing opportunities, the target reuse organisation and the major changes needed to achieve these results.

5 XiosBank

- **Consultant Company:** ATC/UMIST
- **Size of involved team:** medium
- **Domain:** banking
- **Reuse experience:** none
- **Size of application:** big applications
- **Programming language:** Smalltalk
- **Type of software:** client/server sw system
- **Scope:** horizontal
- **Granularity:** Reusable Business Objects
- **Technology:** EUROBANQUET

5.1 Introduction

This report describes the application of a reuse-based software development approach to a pilot project in a bank. The approach is based on the concept of *the reusable banking object* and was applied to XIOSBANK of Greece over the period January-December 1995

5.2 Summary of the Approach

The approach described in this report is based on the concept of a reusable banking object (RBO for short). An RBO is a computer implementation of a banking entity that participates in different transactions across the bank. We define a transaction to be a sequence of events that typically involves the customer and provides a measurable benefit to him/her, e.g. selling a product or service.

The reason we followed this approach, i.e. the business case for applying software reuse in XIOSBANK, is explained in Section 5.3. In summary, the RBO approach can be described as follows:

The RBO approach entails populating a repository of executable reusable software objects (RBOs) The business objects are identified by looking at the various entities (i.e. physical or information entities) that participate in banking transactions and selecting those that have a reuse potential, i.e. are likely to appear also in future transactions. These entities are subsequently implemented in the development environment (workbench) PARTS (a product of Digitalk Inc.) as objects (called *parts* in PARTS terminology). Parts can be put together (assembled) in a visual way (using events and message connections) to form new applications. In the XIOSBANK pilot, RBOs were identified for the area of consumer credit which (as explained in Section 5.3) is of great importance for the bank. These RBOs were implemented as *parts* and classified in catalogues in the PARTS Workbench. Some of the identified RBOs were subsequently reused in the development of a new consumer credit application.

The objectives of this pilot have been as follows:

- To prove that a critical mass of reusable banking objects (RBOs) exists in the consumer credit banking domain.
- To specify the type and level of granularity of such RBOs
- To assess the benefits (if any) from using RBOs in software development, if possible in a quantitative manner.

5.3   The Business Case for Reuse in Xiosbank

XIOSBANK has a strong position in the Greek market of consumer credit (mortgages, personal loans etc.). This is in part due to the fact that in the past, the bank succeeded in many cases to be the first to offer a particular type of credit product and so to capture a large share of the market. To keep and further increase its market share, XIOSBANK's strategy consists of speedily introduction of new products and services taking advantage of opportunities such as for example changes in the Greek legislation for consumer credit. When such changes occur, the bank who gets first to the market with the new product almost always becomes number one in market share.

To support the strategy of rapid new products introduction, XIOSBANK requires the support of an equally rapid application development approach. Such development approach cannot be based on the conventional waterfall model, since this is associated with long development cycles which are unacceptable by the bank. The short lifecycle of a new credit product (as short as two months) for example, implies that the applications required to support it must also be completed within a similar time frame.

A rapid application development (RAD) approach significantly shortens the duration of phases of the waterfall approach such as design, coding and testing. To achieve this, RAD relies on technologies such as visual programming and repositories of software assets.

It is becoming obvious that the business needs of XIOSBANK can only be met by a RAD oriented approach. At the same time it can be argued that the consumer credit domain is rather mature (stable) where most new products are simple variations of a standard theme. This suggests that a stable core of domain knowledge exists for the consumer credit domain and can therefore be reused in the development of new applications. The main conclusion that follows from this line of reasoning is that a RAD approach based on a repository of reusable assets (here called reusable banking objects-RBOs) is required to support the business strategy of XIOSBANK. This pilot was set to (partially) validate this position.

5.3.1 Phases of the Approach

The approach consisted of five steps or phases: 1) Analysis of banking transactions, 2) Identification of common objects across transactions, 3) Selection of a subset of RBOs found in Phase 2, 4) Implementation of RBOs in PARTS workbench, 5) Development of a consumer credit application using RBOs. These phases are explained below.

Phase 1: Analysis of banking transactions. In this phase 5 business transactions corresponding to five consumer credit products were analysed:

- a VISA product,
- a mortgage loan,
- a consumer goods (electrical appliances etc.) loan,
- a home improvement loan,
- a car loan.

The transactions were modelled in terms of collaborating objects (i.e. following similar techniques to the *use case* approach of the OOSE methodology).

Phase 2: Identification of common objects across transactions. In this phase a number of objects participating across all transactions were identified. These correspond to real entities from the banking area (both computer and non-computer-based ones) such as loan officer, loan application form etc.

Phase 3: Selection of a subset of RBOs found in Phase 2. In this phase, a subset of reusable objects found in phase 2 was chosen for implementation in the PARTS environment. The criteria for selecting an RBO were:

1. Its computer implementability. Objects for example like loan officer were not considered to be part of the computer application. Other objects however such as loan application form which were not originally computer-based were selected for computer implementation as it was thought that they could become computer-based in the future development of consumer credit applications.
2. Its reusability content. The motivation behind this pilot has been to develop a repository with assets that can be utilised in the development of future applications. Only objects that were thought to have a role in the development of future applications were selected.

Phase 4: Implementation of RBOs in PARTS workbench. In this phase the chosen RBOs were implemented in the PARTS workbench from Digitalk. Here we provide a partial list of the identified RBOs as well as a more in depth description of a
sample RBO.

5.3.2   Found RBO's

Some of the identified RBOs together with a short description of their functionality
are shown below:

- Repayment_scheduler (creates schedule for loan repayments)
- Credit_scorer (calculates credit worthiness of applicant)
- Address_verifier (verifies that the address supplied by the customer matches the
  one in the address database)
- Interest_calculator (calculates interest repayable given various parameters about
  the loan)

5.4   Findings

The XIOSBANK pilot has proved that a critical mass of reusable components
(RBOs) can be acquired in the consumer credit domain. An RBO is a domain-
specific component which is equivalent to many hundreds of lines of third
generation language code. RBOs consist of lower level domain independent
components such as visual (user interface components) and non-visual (e.g.
computational) ones. In turn, RBOs can be assembled together to deliver
applications. The three layered approach described above is still maturing and
therefore currently lacks large scale empirical validation results. In this section we
present qualitative and quantitative results drawing from the limited experience of
the pilot and from related studies.

5.4.1   Qualitative Benefits

Such benefits result from the impact of the RBO approach on the business strategy
and operations. As argued in Section 5.3, the RBO approach supports a business
strategy that is based on the rapid introduction of new products. It was also said in
the same section that the speed with which the bank responds to changing market
conditions by introducing new products is essential for market dominance. In this
sense the business benefits of the RBO, although difficult to quantify, can be
tremendous corresponding to the financial gains associated with capturing a market
share.

In addition, benefits can be attributed to the ability of RBOs to address the
business needs for computer support in a meaningful to the end-users way. Since
they are abstractions of real world entities, RBOs are easily understood to the

banking users and provide therefore the basis for specifying requirements or for interacting with in applications.

5.4.2 Quantifiable Benefits

Quantifiable benefits from the use of information technology applications are in general difficult to derive under most circumstances. In this section we present a number of simple mathematical formulas that can be used for calculating savings as the result of applying RBOs at different stages of application development in an organisation. Most of the values for the parameters used to calculate the benefits have been taken from the literature. It is possible however to substitute some of the values with others more representative of the type of application, development approach etc. of a particular organisation, when such data are available.

The benefits have been classified under the system development activities of application scoping, requirements definition, design and construction.

Application Scoping Benefit: When asked to scope an application business representatives can more easily pinpointed its scope by referring to RBOs This provides a fast and accurate definition of the application's boundary. Significant changes can accrue in two ways: First, time it takes to define the business scope of the application is reduced. Second, the accuracy of the scoping reduces the maintenance load caused by need to add additional business functionality which would have been present in the application on its first release.

The application scopingbenefit can be calxulated according to the following formula:

(IS budget
* percentage of IS Budget applied to application development
* percentage of application development applied to scoping
* time saved by availability of RBO)
+
(IS budget
* percentage of IS budget applied to maintenance
* percentage of maintenance cost allocated to adding additional functionality
* reduction in redundant functionality due to RBO).

For example, the following data:

- Application development budget of $1M per year,
- 60% of budget applied to development of new IS,
- 10% of it applied to application scoping,
- 50% time saving because of availability of RBOs,
- 40% of budget applied to maintenance of IS,
- 70% of maintenance cost applied to additional functionality,
- 20% improvement in accuracy of application scoping,

yields a value for benefit1 of $1M * 0.6 * 0.1 *0.5 + $1M * 0.4 * 0.7 * 0.2 = $86000.

Requirements Definition Benefit: The RBO approach provides accurate input to requirements definition and helps in two ways: First, it reduces user participation time and business analysis time. Second, improves the productivity of the requirements phase by reusing requirements. Therefore,

The requirements definition benefit may be calculated according to the following formula:

(IS Budget
* Percentage of IS budget applied to application development
* percentage of application development time applied to requirements definition
* time saved by applying RBOs)
+
(IS Budget
* Percentage of IS budget applied to application development
* percentage of application development time applied to requirements definition
* time saved by reusing requirements from RBO)

For example the following data:

- Application development budget of $1M per year,
- 60% of budget applied to development of new IS,
- 20% of application development time applied to requirements definition,
- 20% reduction in requirements definition time due to use of RBO,
- 50% reduction in requirements definition time by reusing requirements,

yields savingsof : $1M * 0.6 *0.2 * 0.2 + $1M * 0.6 * 0.2 * 0.5 = $84000

Design and Construction Benefits: The following benefits come under design and construction:

a. Productivity increase due to shared entity (database) objects. This has shown to reduce programming time by 20 to 40 percent.
b. Reusability of business objects (interface, control and entity objects). Entity objects (files, databases) have the highest degree of reusability, followed by interface objects (forms, reports), followed by control objects. Assuming that in a typical application, 60% of the objects are entity objects, 30% are interface objects and 10% control objects, and also assuming that their degrees of reusability are 80%, 40% and 20% respectively leads to an average degree of reusability of approximately 62%.

Therefore for design and construction, wemay calculate the benefit as:

(Information Systems Budget
* Percentage of IS budget applied to application development
* percentage of IS budget applied to construction
* estimated productivity increase made possible by reuse of data specifications
* estimated% contribution to data sharing made possible by RBO approach)
+

(Information Systems Budget
* Percentage of IS budget applied to application development
* percentage of IS budget applied to construction
* average degree of reuse in an application
* estimated productivity gains achieved by reuse of objects)

For example the following data:

- Application development budget of $1M per year.
- 60% of budget applied to development of new IS.
- 30% of application development time applied to design and construction.
- 30% productivity increase made possible by shared database specifications
- 60% contribution to data sharing made possible by RBOs
- 62% average degree of reusability in an application
- 50% productivity gains achieved by reuse of objects

yields: $1M * 0.6 *0.3 *0.3 * 0.6 + $1M * 0.6 * 0.3 * 0.62 *0.5 = $88200

By adding together the benefits calculated above we arrive at a total benefit of $258200 which is roughly equal to 43% of the budget for development of new applications.

5.5   Conclusions

To recall from Section 5.1, the main objectives of this pilot have been:

1. To prove that there exist reusable banking objects (RBOs) in the consumer credit banking domain.
2. To specify the type and level of granularity of such RBOs
3. To assess the benefits from using RBOs (if any) if possible in a quantitative manner.

Objective number 1 has been clearly met: a number of RBOs (over 20) has been developed, providing the critical mass required for reuse-based application development.

Objective number 2 has also been realised since analysis of various banking transactions within the consumer credit area provided indications about the type and granularity of RBOs. More specifically, the findings of this pilot indicate that RBOs should be rather fine granularity objects such as *interest calculator* rather than coarse granularity ones such as *customer, account* etc. It was found that more general objects such as customer, account etc., although useful for analysis tasks they were far too large and complicated to be directly reusable in an executable format. With regard to the nature of RBOs it was found that they are predominantly information resources that are employed by the decision makers in the bank (e.g. customer information) or implement simple banking policies and procedures

Objective 3 is the most difficult to assess due to the limited nature of the pilot both in terms of duration (less than 12 months) and available resources. The pilot has indicated that there are measurable benefits associated with the RBO approach in terms of productivity improvement. As the RBO approach has been implemented using the PARTS environment it becomes difficult to isolate benefits which are purely a result of reusability from those which are due to other features of the PARTS environment (e.g. visual construction of user interface).

In conclusion, the RBO approach seems to meet the requirements of today's banks, i.e. to provide an application architecture that supports the business processes and strategy. More real life experimentation is needed to quantify the benefits of the approach.

6 Stentofon[1]

- **Consultant Company:** SINTEF
- **Size of involved team:** 20
- **Domain:** intercom
- **Reuse experience:** some
- **Size of application:** 300,000 LOC
- **Programming language:** C+SDL
- **Type of software:** embedded
- **Scope:** product line / vertical
- **Granularity:** O-O framework
- **Technology:** PROTEUS

6.1 Introduction

The work described in this section is carried out in the scope of PROTEUS, project number 6086 in the European Commission ESPRIT research and development programme. The work carried out in Norway has been partly funded by the Norwegian Research Council (NFR).

Stentofon is an industrial company based in Trondheim, Norway. Their principal business is the production of customised internal intercom systems. They design and supply both the hardware and the software elements of these systems, and are a market leader in this area.

Stentofon has been in this business for many years, and has a significant share of the world market for this type of product. As a result, they have a large number of installations around the world - and many of these are different variants of the intercom product. Good hardware reliability also means that many older systems are still in use. In addition, it has always been - and continues to be - an important element of company strategy that Stentofon provides *customised* solutions for the special needs of individual customers. Combined with the large number of

---

installations, this means that the company is responsible for the maintenance and further development of a very large variety of systems.

The large variety of systems produced by Stentofon, combined with the fact that new product development is always necessary to maintain a competitive edge, means that support for evolving systems is very important at Stentofon. Although evolution applies to both the hardware and software parts of the product, the issues discussed in this paper will be restricted to the software components.

6.1.1   Tool Chain for Software Development

The tool chain used at Stentofon is summarised in Fig. 6.1. It is mainly based on use of the design language SDL [ITU93], supported by a methodology [Bræ93] developed in the SISU[2] programme. Software development is carried out on a host environment consisting of a network of workstations; code developed on that platform is then re-generated for various target platforms consisting of the hardware systems developed by Stentofon.

SDL is a high-level specification language with a graphical syntax which facilitates communication amongst system designers and between them and the customer. It is highly suitable for expressing the functional design of real-time software systems of the type developed by Stentofon, and provides a clear picture of system structure and behaviour. For editing and analysing SDL descriptions, Stentofon use the SDT toolset [SDT95]. The support offered by this toolset is satisfactory, but there is very limited support for handling variants of systems.

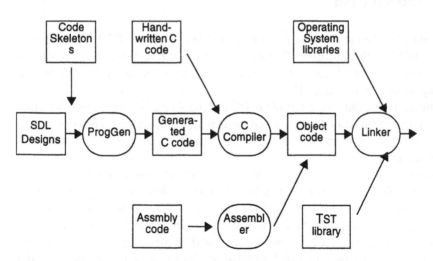

Fig. 6.1. SDL tool chain used at Stentofon.

---

[2] SISU is a Norwegian national research and development programme (1988-1996). Its main goal is to increase the effectiveness of software production for the real-time software industry in Norway.

SDL is not a 'programming' language, and there are many different strategies one might choose to implement designs expressed in SDL [Gor91]. There is no single, obvious strategy for producing implementations from SDL descriptions. Nevertheless - to support evolution - it is best to work at as high an abstraction level as possible, without being too concerned about implementation strategies. The Stentofon approach to this problem is to *transform* SDL designs to C code, in such a flexible way that the system designer can describe/select the transformations that are appropriate as the system evolves. For this purpose, the ProgGen tool [Flo95] from SINTEF is used.

ProgGen has two inputs: the SDL description to be transformed and a set of *code skeletons* which allow the designer to describe the exact strategy for transformation to C to be used in a particular case. By using this automatic but flexible code generation, the advantages of working at the SDL level can be maintained, while still maintaining flexibility at the programming language level. Using this approach, about 75% of the system functionality in the Stentofon systems is maintained at the SDL level. However, various practical considerations mean that some parts of the software have to be directly coded in C or (in a few cases) in assembler.

SDL is based on the concept of finite state machines (FSMs) which execute in parallel, and communicate by exchanging signals. Thus, efficient implementations of SDL systems are usually based on use of an SDL *run-time system* providing low-level implementation support for the high-level SDL concepts. Stentofon uses the TST product [TST95] for this purpose. TST provides an SDL run-time system consisting of a library of support routines, together with extensive test facilities. In order to use TST, it is necessary to provide a set of *configuration files* which include information like which SDL processes will execute on which physical processors.

6.1.2 Variability

The tool chain described above has proven to be effective at Stentofon, and the advantages of working as much as possible at the SDL level are appreciated by all members of the software development team. However, there are many different types of 'source code' that have to be carefully managed:

- SDL designs
- ProgGen skeletons for describing the process of C code generation
- C code and Assembly code, hand-written
- TST configuration description files
- declaration of the system building process, currently represented by a set of shell script files and makefiles
- 'foreign' libraries, e.g. TST, AMX etc.

As the system evolves, variants of all of these item types are produced, and dependencies between them also increase in complexity. To make effective use of the various tools of the development platform, it is vital that support be provided to control these sources of variability.

6.2   Support Needed by Stentofon

This section describes the problems concerning evolution that Stentofon identified *before* the PROTEUS project started. In each sub-section, we describe the nature of the problem, the requirements for improved support and 'Today's approach' i.e. how the problems are currently being handled *without* support from PROTEUS. In Section 6.4 we assess the extent to which these problems have been solved or alleviated by using the PROTEUS approach.

6.2.1   General Requirements

Stentofon requires support for two main *types* of system evolution: evolution over *time* (corrections, product enhancements, adaptations for new platforms etc.) and evolution arising from *customisations* carried out for specific customers. The support provided must handle *revisions and variants* of all the item types involved in the tool chain described in Section 6.1.1. In particular, it has to be able to deal with:

- stable system versions: systems already delivered to customers
- versions under development (including test and debug variants)
- variants for different platforms (host/target)
- variants produced to fulfil the needs of specific customers.

A basic requirement is to provide *visibility* of the overall system structure, clearly indicating which parts of the system are common and which vary. For variants it must be possible to express that the choice for one item might depend on the choice of variant for some other items.

Another key issue is support for the *system building* process. Since this process is to a large extent determined by the system structure, consistency between these must be ensured. The build process should:

- be completely automated, through tool support
- result in executable code that is at least as time and space efficient as that previously produced using a less automated generation process
- be reliable: *all* necessary re-compilations etc. needed for a new variant must be carried out using the correct versions of files, compiler flags etc.
- be fast: unnecessary build operations must be avoided.

Today's approach: Existing support for evolution falls far short of the requirements described above. There is no globally documented, detailed overview of existing system variants, so 'visibility' is poor. RCS [TICc85] is used for version control of the various types of source files, and Make [FEL79] is used for partial automation of the system building process.

6.2.2 SDL Composition Structure

Systems described in SDL are essentially built up of *processes* and *procedures* which are composed in a hierarchical *block* structure. In developing evolving systems, Stentofon often wish to reuse particular processes, procedures and block hierarchies; these elements need to be composed to produce a given system variant. However, the version of the SDL language used by Stentofon lacks support for modularisation[3], and composition must be carried out using various ad hoc facilities provided by the SDT editor tool.

This composition problem is particularly important because the SDL level is the 'top' level of the system, and many other components used to generate an executable system are dependent on the SDL composition structure.

Stentofon require tool support which facilitates composition of SDL processes etc. into complete SDL systems. Systems composed in this way must then be able to be used as the basis for the automated system generation process, in full confidence that all dependencies with other item types (C code, ProgGen skeletons etc.) will be taken into account.

Today's approach: SDL composition is carried out using the SDL editor provided in the SDT tool; this involves a considerable degree of user interaction, and makes it very difficult to see which variants of which SDL components are composed together in different system variants.

6.2.3 Complexity of System Generation

The system building process used at Stentofon involves many complex dependencies between the various item types that are involved in the process. These have to be taken into account when deciding which tool invocations are necessary, as do other sources of variability such as the correct compiler flags etc. that are needed when generating a particular system instance.

The process is made more complex because it is necessary to translate from SDL to C: there is a large number of ProgGen skeletons (several hundred), and it is essential that the skeletons used during system generation are appropriate for the system variant being produced. Skeletons must be selected according to which translation strategies are required to fulfil the functional and non-functional requirements of a particular delivery.

Given the general requirement that system generation should be completely automated, tool support is required which takes account of these complexities and ensures consistent choices.

Today's approach: System building is performed using a mixture of makefiles and shell scripts. The 'implicit' rules provided by Make have proven not to be sufficiently powerful to handle the complexities of the system generation process,

---

[3] Stentofon currently use SDL/88. Section 6.5.1 discusses possible consequences of converting to SDL/92.

and a considerable amount of manual maintenance of makefiles is necessary. This is both time-consuming and potentially error prone. It has also led to a situation where the flexibility offered by the Proggen skeleton mechanism has not been fully exploited because of the complexities of selection of skeletons during system generation.

6.2.4   Run-time System and Operating System Considerations

Some important sources of variability are dealt with at the run-time support and operating system level. For particular system variants, customisations are needed in order to make most effective use of the basic hardware/software platform on which the system will run.

A case in point is the *distribution* of the software: which SDL processes will run on which physical processors? This is dealt with by producing appropriate low-level *configuration* files for the TST run-time support system.

Tool support is required which will remove the need to maintain such low level files, and allow such considerations as software distribution to be dealt with at a higher abstraction level.

Today's approach: No tool support: all dependencies are dealt with by manual procedures.

6.3   The PROTEUS Approach

The objective of the PROTEUS project was to provide support for system evolution. The project has developed methods and tools for domain analysis, for adapting existing design methods (SDL, HOOD, MD and OORAM) to support evolving systems, and for modelling system structure and software system building. Stentofon participated as an application company in PROTEUS.

6.3.1   PROTEUS Configuration Language (PCL)

PCL [Proteus94] is a formalism for system modelling and software system building. As systems evolve, large numbers of system and component versions with slightly different properties are created. A *system model* is a description of the items in a system and the relationships between them. Such a model uniquely identifies the comprising components, their properties and structure, and tracks their evolution. Variability should be represented, making it clear what is common and what differs between system variants. Its purpose is to capture knowledge about a system and its domain in an understandable and concise manner.

The system model in PCL is based on the *family* notion. A family represents a logical entity which may occur in different variations in particular systems. The family description encompasses all potential variability of the entity. A specific member (version) of the family is determined by removing ambiguity in the family description. We call this operation *binding*, and it is one of the core functions of the tool set supporting PCL usage.

6.3.2 System Modelling Facilities

In PCL the **family** construct is used for modelling the logical entities in the system. A model is organised as a layered composition structure at the logical level. Entities may be part of other entities, and may also have sub-components. In the **parts** section the logical composition structure is declared. The following example shows ASVP[4] – one of the sub-systems in the Stentofon application.

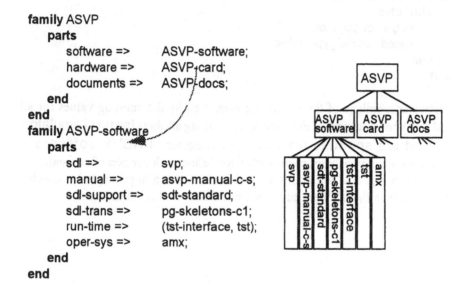

```
family ASVP
    parts
        software =>      ASVP-software;
        hardware =>      ASVP-card;
        documents =>     ASVP-docs;
    end
end
family ASVP-software
    parts
        sdl =>           svp;
        manual =>        asvp-manual-c-s;
        sdl-support =>   sdt-standard;
        sdl-trans =>     pg-skeletons-c1;
        run-time =>      (tst-interface, tst);
        oper-sys =>      amx;
    end
end
```

In the example above, the **ASVP** entity is composed of **ASVP-software**, **ASVP-card** and **ASVP-docs**. The decomposition of **ASVP-software** is further indicated. Parts may of course be shared among subsystems, relationships which must be kept track of during change impact analysis.

A family may represent any kind of entity: hardware objects, software artifacts or even combinations. PCL facilitates multi-dimensional classification in user-defined term spaces. There is also a **relationships** section for declaring other kinds of relationships between entities and a general **relation** definition facility.

Attributes are used to characterise a family and its potential variability. Attributes are typed and may be of type integer, string, or a user-defined enumeration. There are two kinds of attributes, information attributes and variability control attributes. Information attributes state properties common to all members of the family. They are declared by using the '=' assignment operator.

---

[4] ASVP is an abbreviation for AICE Stored Voice Playback.

```
family hwif-manual-c
   attributes
       language: string = "C";
   end
end
```

Variability control attributes indicate possible variability among the members of a family. Default values may be assigned to such attributes with the ':=' operator, but these may be overridden at binding time.

```
family ASVP-software
   attributes
       target : target_type;
       speed : speed_type := fast;
   end
end
```

Particular members of the family are identified by determining values for all variability control attributes. For example, if binding attribute **target** to **emulator-stripped** and **speed** to **fast,** a unique member of **ASVP-software** is established. Each variability control attribute defines a dimension of variability as illustrated in Fig. 6.2. Variability control attributes can in principle be selected independently, although there might be some disallowed combinations.

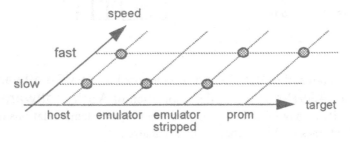

Fig. 6.2. Two Dimensions of Variability and Some Possible Family Members

Note that attributes denote *conceptual* variability – they do not say anything about how that variability is realised. PCL covers a wide range of types of variability, for example structural variability, version selection of associated physical objects, and differences in processing tool parameters. The example below illustrates *structural* variability, i.e. a family whose members have different composition structures. This is expressed by embedding **if-then-else** phrases in the description. Such phrases use expressions based on attribute values. Alternatives can also be viewed graphically as illustrated in Fig. 6.3.

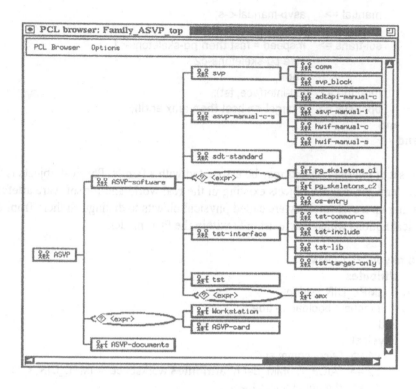

Fig. 6.3. PCL Browser View of Top Levels of ASVP.

```
family ASVP
    attributes
        target : target_type;
    end
    parts
        software =>   ASVP-software;
        hardware =>   if target = host then
                          Workstation
                      else ASVP-card
                      endif;
        documents =>ASVP-docs;
    end
end

family ASVP-software
    attributes
        target : target_type;
        speed : speed_type;
    end
    parts
        sdl =>        svp;
```

```
        manual =>    asvp-manual-c-s;
        sdl-support =>sdt-standard;
        sdl-trans =>   if speed = fast then pg-skeletons-c1
                       else pg-skeletons-c2
                       endif;
        run-time =>   (tst-interface, tst);
        oper-sys =>   if target <> host then amx endif;
    end
  end
```

A set of *physical objects* may be associated with a family. Physical objects is the PCL term for tangible objects existing in the real world and for software artefacts making up a system. They are called physical objects to distinguish them from the logical notions which may exist only within the PCL model.

```
family AICE_COMM
    attributes
        IMPL_DIR : string;
        manual : boolean := true;
    end
    physical
        p1 => "aice_comm.spr";
        p2 => "AICE_COMM_def.h" attributes workspace := IMPL_DIR; end;
        p3 => if manual = true then
                  "AICE_COMM_proc.c"
                  attributes workspace := IMPL_DIR; end
              endif;
    end
  end
```

Three physical objects named aice_comm.spr, AICE_COMM_def.h and AICE_COMM_proc.c are associated with the AICE_COMM entity representing an SDL process. Attributes and classifications may be declared for physical objects just as for families. All physical objects here are software objects, i.e. files, which is the default unless classified otherwise. The **workspace** attribute is a special attribute recognised by the PCL tools which indicates where in the file system this file should reside.

In descriptions of large systems, it often happens that several family descriptions share a similar structure and content. In Stentofon's ASVP system, for example, one family description is required for each SDL process in the system. It would be tedious to have to write (basically) the same PCL description once for each SDL process; it would also be difficult to maintain all the descriptions. To avoid such problems, PCL provides a comprehensive *inheritance* mechanism. Thus, for Stentofon's ASVP system, one can capture the *common* information in an **sdl-process** family, and highlight what is *unique* to each individual process in separate family descriptions all of which inherit from **sdl-process**.

As mentioned previously, a particular member of a family is determined by assigning values to the variability control attributes. Such attribute assignments are specified in a *version descriptor*. These will override the default expressions occurring in the family model.

```
version v-ASVP-host of ASVP-software
    attributes
        target := host;
        speed := slow;
        HOME := "/users/arvid/";
    end
end
```

During binding the version descriptor is applied to the family and sub-families recursively, producing a bound family hierarchy. If a version descriptor is incomplete (i.e. a value is not specified for all variability control attributes), a partially bound family will result. This corresponds to a partially bound configuration.

To handle the problem of file versions, we have chosen a two-tier repository approach. The contents and the descriptions of file versions are managed by a special tool called the Repository. Otherwise, descriptions of file versions would soon make the system model impracticably voluminous and hard to use.

Version selection is the process of determining a consistent set of versions for elements of a system. PCL supports intentional version selection [BEL86]. Based on a query stating desired properties, the best matching version (if any) for each file is computed by the Repository by inspecting the available versions and their characteristics. This process is controlled by the PCL system model, since the submitted query is constructed by including certain attributes from the PCL model. Details of this are outside the scope of this paper.

6.3.3 System Building Support

For modelling software system building processes, PCL includes the **tool** construct. It allows declarative specifications of steps in the building process by defining the signature and behaviour of software tools. A C compiler may be modelled as follows:

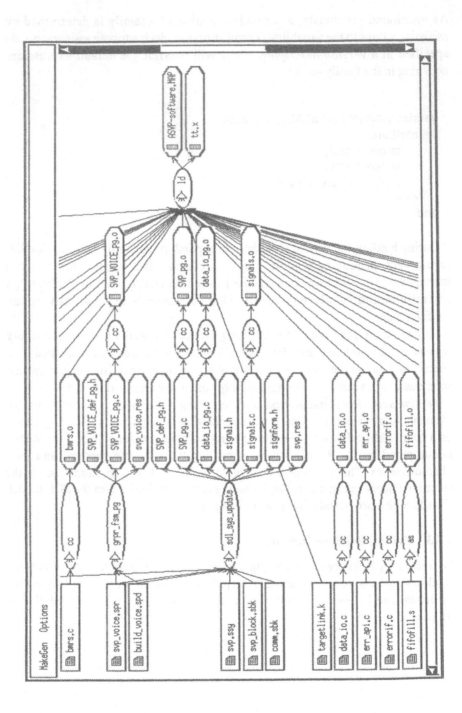

Fig. 6.4. Derivation Graph Produced During Makefile Generation.

```
tool cc
    attributes
        CC : string default "cc ";
        CFLAGS : string default " ";
        CINCL : string default " ";
    end
    inputs in =>  c-source; end
    outputs out =>obj-68k; end
    scripts
        build :=   CC ++ CFLAGS ++ CINCL ++ "-o " ++ out ++ " -c " ++ in;
    end
end
```

The input and output sections specify that this derivation step template transforms a file classified as **c-source** into a **obj-68k** file.

The **build** script specifies the actual command line for tool invocation. It is also possible to describe more complex tools, with multiple inputs and outputs.

System building support in PROTEUS is currently realised by generating standard makefiles, which are interpreted by the Make program [FEL79] for actual system (re)generation. Fig. 6.4. shows a part of the derivation graph for an **ASVP-software** variant. The generated makefiles may optionally include check-out rules of correct versions of file

6.3.4   Tool Support

A comprehensive toolset to support the creation and use of PCL models has been developed. Fig. 6.5. presents an overview of the core PCL tool set.

- *PCL compiler* is an interactive tool for management and analysis of PCL models. Primarily it supports the three fundamental operations for PCL models, namely binding, version selection, and makefile generation. Partial and interactive binding are both supported. Some other functionality is available as well, e.g. parsing and unparsing of textual PCL descriptions, check-in and check-out of software subsystems to/from the Repository.
- *PCL editor/browser* is a graphical structural editor for entering and browsing PCL models.
- The *Repository* manages the contents and descriptions (attribute annotations) of versions of software objects.
- *Repository browser* is a graphical browser for inspecting and manipulating the contents of the Repository.
- The *PCL reverse* tool allows automatic construction of rudimentary PCL models for existing software systems. It also includes features to perform consistency checks between the workspace, the Repository and a PCL model for the software parts of a system.

6.4   The PROTEUS Approach Applied in Stentofon

In this section we discuss how the PROTEUS approach may be integrated into Stentofon's development process. The discussion is organised according to the requirements for evolution support listed in Section 6.2.

6.4.1   General Requirements

Overall system *visibility* is provided by the PCL system model. Descriptions of all relevant parts and their inter-dependencies are possible, for e.g. SDL parts, hand-coded software, documentation, hardware elements. Elements are classified in a company-defined schema. The system building process is controlled from the same descriptions, ensuring consistency between the model and the actually generated system.

The PCL system model allows representation of all potential variability in a system, highlighting which parts are common and which differ between variants. In Stentofon a number of different mechanisms for achieving software variability are used, e.g.:

- varying system composition
- component selection, i.e. different files
- component version selection (revisions and branches)
- conditional text inclusion (*conditional compilation*)

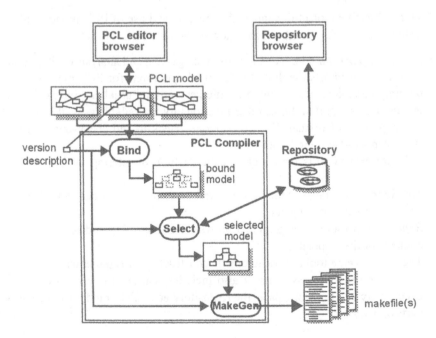

Fig. 6.5. Tool Overview

- tool selection and ordering of invocation
- tool parameters/switches, e.g. for selection of code generation skeletons, target platform, debug support, optimisation
- configuration files for the run-time system.

PCL allows expressing and controlling variability of all these kinds with a single mechanism, namely attributes. Dependencies between variability selections may also be expressed.

6.4.2 SDL Composition Structure

The SDL decomposition structure is reflected in the PCL model. Each SDL system, block, process and procedure is described by a PCL family construct, which includes references to the SDL source and associated handwritten-code (if any). Initially this PCL fragment is created by running ProgGen on the initial SDL model with an appropriate set of skeletons. After subsequent *structural* changes at the SDL level, these must be incorporated into the system model by a manual merge step using the PCL editor. This task typically involves inserting conditional expressions over attributes and possibly introducing new attributes. For structural changes in the hand-written code, i.e. creation or removal of files, a similar procedure is followed, but now PCL reverse may be used to produce the PCL fragment to merge into the existing model.

To generate a particular system instance, a user states the desired properties related to functional characteristics, non-functional aspects, implementation choices etc. in the form of a version descriptor. During the instantiation process the best matching SDL component versions are selected, possibly forming an original combination of versions. The SDT tool [SDT95] reports any inconsistencies, and allows manual editing to resolve conflicts if necessary.

6.4.3 Complexity of System Generation

PCL allows all knowledge related to the system building process to be stated in one formalism and be represented in one place. Complex derivation steps far exceeding the expressiveness of implicit Make rules [FEL85] are handled. Manual maintenance of makefiles and shell scripts is avoided by automatically generating appropriate makefiles for each particular system instance.

To ease maintenance of the system model itself, *derived* relationships are supported in PCL. Dependencies which are possible to derive from files, e.g. #include dependencies between C source code files, need not be represented in the system model. By rather declaring **depend** scripts for **tool** entities, such dependencies may be automatically extracted during the system building process. Variability in the SDL-to-C transformation is solved by including a model of the ProgGen skeleton set as a subsystem of the system model. Skeleton files are versioned and managed by the Repository. Variability in this subsystem is then characterised and disambiguated just as any other variability in the system model.

6.4.4   Runtime System and Operating System Considerations

The runtime organisation of an application is possible to model in PCL. PCL includes predefined relations which are taken into account during system analysis, allowing a high-level declaration of distribution aspects and usage of the underlying platform. Since hardware elements are already included in the model, this fits naturally into the framework.

However, the ultimate goal of automatically generating appropriate TST low-level configuration files from such a PCL model has not yet been achieved. We hope to be able to express this generation step using the general **tool** construct, but some technical problems still remain.

6.5   Evaluation

This section reports on experiences from applying the PROTEUS approach at Stentofon. Table 6.1. shows the number of files, total number of lines of code, and number of versions per. file. Totally there were 721 manually maintained files and over 8000 versions of these. Note that all *generated* files (C files generated from SDL, Make dependency files, etc.) are omitted.

Table 6.1. Size Metrics for the Stentofon AICE Application

Type of source	No. of files	LOC	Versions pr. file
SDL	141	181421[a]	5-300
C	238	93500	10-100
Assembly	14	5266	10-100
Configuration files	11	918	5-50
ProgGen skeletons	288	3481	2-5
Foreign libraries	2		3-5
Makefiles, shell scripts	27	17224[b]	10-100

[a] LOC for SDL source is approximated by the number of bytes in GR files divided by 30.
[b] Five of these makefiles (14.263 LOC) are for recreation of old configurations.

Table 6.2. gives the size of the PCL model of the AICE application. When using the PROTEUS approach 'Makefiles/shell scripts' and possibly 'Configuration files' in Table 6.1. can be eliminated, since they will be generated automatically from the PCL model.

Table 6.2. PCL Model

Type of source	No. of files	LOC
Generic[a]	3	500
System specific[b]	7	1700

[a.] Common to all SDL-based systems in Stentofon
[b.] Of this ca. 75% was initially generated by ProgGen.

The evaluation has been based on three main criteria: (1) support for evolutionary development, (2) support for design-oriented development, and (3) flexibility of approach. Among the more advantageous experiences we can mention:

- PCL allows a number of tasks to be done at higher abstraction level than before. Many highly inter-dependent details around the system and in the associated system building process are now automatically taken care of based on intentional specifications.
- Constructing a *total* system model covering all aspects of a system has been a favourable experience. Knowledge previously distributed and unavailable (person dependent) is now made visible and represented in a formal model. This information is also useful e.g. for internal communication and training. Modelling of system variability is however still somewhat incomplete.
- The choice of building the Repository on top of an existing version management system has been quite fortunate at Stentofon. Several years of evolution history are instantly available, presented in a graphical user interface.
- 'High' expressiveness of PCL is a vital factor for the success of PCL. It allows concise models, which are easy to understand and maintain as the system evolves. Intentional mechanisms are essential to handle the size and complexity of real systems.

Problem areas and deficiencies observed are:

- A crucial problem is to ensure consistency between the system model and the actual system. Structural and even some non-structural changes require that the system model is updated. More tight integration between the design tool and the PCL model is one possibility, currently being explored by other partners in PROTEUS.
- A more practical obstacle in the experimentation has been the lack of availability, stability and maturity of the PCL toolset. The tools were originally released for a platform not available at Stentofon's development department.
- Fully automatic generation of run-time system configuration files not yet achieved.

6.5.1   Looking Ahead: SDL/92

This evaluation is based on use of the SDL/88 version of SDL, which is the one currently in use at Stentofon. However, as tool support for SDL/92 is now becoming available, Stentofon will almost certainly start using SDL/92 in the near future. While we obviously cannot here report on experiences of using ProgGen and the PCL tools in conjunction with SDL/92, it is worthwhile considering the impact that the change to SDL/92 is likely to have. From a software engineering perspective, SDL/92 offers the following main advantages over SDL/88:

- easier to modularise, using *types* and *packages;*
- variants can be described using *inheritance;*
- possible to produce more generic descriptions, using *context parameters.*

These improvements in the language make it easier to structure system descriptions, and to handle variability as systems evolve. However, we do not believe that these new language facilities are sufficient to provide the support for evolution required in an industrial context. In fact, the use of inheritance can actually complicate management of the system descriptions through the extra dependencies that are introduced, and the wider range of translation strategies that become possible.

In conclusion, our expectation is that use of SDL/92 will improve our software development process, but that the support provided by the ProgGen translation tool and the PCL toolset will, in total, be no less beneficial when using SDL/92 than when using SDL/88.

6.6   Conclusions

Software is a valuable organisational asset. As organisations find themselves having to respond more and more quickly to business and environmental changes, it is important that the collective expertise and knowledge about a system can be pooled, formalised and recorded. Although formal description techniques as SDL significantly reduces the size of the system representations, the large number of source elements to manage and the complex building processes in industrial systems necessitates method and tool support.

Using PCL to support evolution through the use of complete system models is a promising approach to this problem. Experience at Stentofon shows that it requires a significant effort to build such models, but that the benefits in terms of improved visibility and automation are also substantial.

The initial experience reported here is sufficiently positive that Stentofon intends to continue this evaluation work, and it is quite likely that they will eventually decide to adopt PCL in all their software development projects. The potential *economic* benefit of the evolution support provided by PROTEUS has not been assessed by the work reported here. It is an important issue, and future work based on longer-term evaluations should be planned.

7 Garex[1]

- **Consultant Company:** SINTEF
- **Size of involved team:** 30
- **Domain:** communication
- **Reuse experience:** a lot
- **Size of application:** 500 KLOC
- **Programming language:** C
- **Type of software:** embedded
- **Scope:** product-line/vertical
- **Granularity:** O-O frameworks
- **Technology:** PROTEUS/REBOOT

7.1 Introduction

Garex makes customised communication control systems. Garex has been in this market segment since the company was started, and has long experience in making such safety-critical applications. In order to keep development costs down, a standardised software architecture and extensive reuse of (software) components have been employed for numerous years. Their business success is highly dependent on high-quality, reliable, and thoroughly tested basic components.

Over time the software components have become very flexible, i.e. they allow tailoring to a wide range of operating contexts. This has been the result of a deliberate policy in Garex.

Due to extreme availability requirements, it must be possible to modify many of these parameters while the system is running. Binding flexibility at e.g. compile-time cannot therefore be used. A general mechanism for controlling component variability and connectivity is built into the general architecture and a *configuration file* containing parameter values and other information is used for controlling component behaviour and intercommunication. For real applications, such

---

configuration files become quite large, and they are hard to create and modify due to many interdependencies.

This Chapter reports on some practical work undertaken to assess the use of a formalised configuration language for describing components, their potential flexibility and possible composition. The PROTEUS configuration language (PCL) is a formalism for defining system models, including information on all sources of variability within the system. Declarative specification of the associated system building process is also provided. PCL is supported by editing, analysis and system generation tools.

Section 7.2 and Section 7.3 start with a description of the industrial context and the current problem areas in Garex' development and system release processes. In Section 7.4 the PROTEUS approach to system development and re-engineering is outlined. The following section discusses how the approach was applied in Garex, and includes fragments of PCL code to illustrate how problems from Section 7.3 were addressed. Finally, Section 7.6 provides an assessment on how successful the approach has proven to be in its practical application in Garex.

7.2   Industrial Context

7.2.1   GAREX

Garex is a subsidiary of the Norwegian Telecom and employ approximately 50 people. The company is located in Oslo, Norway and has a long history in the professional communication market.

Garex produces Voice Communication Control Switch systems (i.e. systems used for control through voice) to the professional communication control market. The systems provides reliable and effective voice communication services in the professional control and command market as Air Traffic Control, Sea Traffic, Rescue Coordination, Vessel Traffic Management and Police. More than 50 systems have been installed around the world. Several international airports in Europe are among the major customers.

Some of the basic functionality of the delivered systems is the same, but the customers require different communication services and use different special network solutions. They also have very strong opinions about the detailed operations. An important aspect of Garex strategy is then to provide highly customised systems i.e. systems which solve the particular needs of a customer.

Although Garex designs and supplies both the software and hardware elements of the systems, the issues discussed here is restricted to software components. The hardware parts of the product are quite stable, while large parts of the software evolve continuously. Garex uses a software implementation methodology that facilitates product evolution and reuse. This methodology and the tool support need to be enhanced.

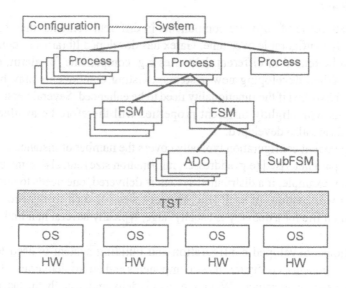

Fig. 7.1. Implemented System

7.2.2 Software Architecture

Garex software runs on the runtime support system TST [TST95]. TST enforces a particular software architecture as shown on Figure 7.1., which has proven very well suited for Garex' application domain. TST concepts have a strong influence on the way of thinking about problems, of modelling systems, and of designing programs at Garex.

TST allows the developer to realise FSM[2]-based distributed software systems. TST provides a library of support routines which implement the communication mechanisms between FSMs and the interpretation of the FSM state transition tables, but also it defines structural, functional and data entity types:

- FSMs are the active components in the system.
- Processes are containers for one or more FSMs
- SubFSMs are similar to procedures in programming languages. They have states.
- ADOs (Abstract Data Objects) offer support for organizing and hiding data and their associated operations.

Standardisation of the component types and interfaces provided by TST facilitate reuse of the components across systems. An important aspect of TST is to support system and component configuration: at system start-up and during operation TST reads a system configuration file.

---

[2] Finite State Machine

7.2.3 Reuse

To facilitate reuse of software components in different contexts, they have been made highly configurable over time. Garex has developed libraries of components which can be reused in different deliveries e.g. components for alarm, operator, statistics. When developing new systems, existing components may be reused directly or reworked if the functionality need to be enhanced. Several versions of the components with slightly different properties will therefore be available. New components are also developed.

The component configuration typically covers the number of instances, how each instance is parameterised (e.g. addresses, information size) and also some behaviour choices. For example, if a distributed system is delivered, one needs to describe the number of workstations of each type, memory sizes of each workstation etc. The configuration file for a delivery is usually huge, typically several hundred kilobytes of text.

An in-house developed configuration and building system is used to select[3] product components, configure[4] these components and build[5] deliveries. Garex uses RCS for version management. When a system is delivered, usually the last approved versions of the source code files are selected. A delivery log file describes the versions which are used. The log file can be used later for reproducing delivered systems.

7.3   Problem Areas

This section describes problem areas identified in the current software development process in Garex, i.e. before introduction of the PROTEUS approach. In Section 7.5, we outline how and assess to what extent these problems have been solved or alleviated by using PROTEUS technology.

7.3.1   High-level Modelling and System Variability

The major drawback in the practice of reuse and configuration at Garex is the lack of a high level model of the complete product and its potential variability. Components are not well documented and reuse relies heavily on the knowledge of a small kernel of developers:

---

[3] The selection is done partially manually based on the developers knowledge of the existing component types.

[4] The configuration can be generated partially automatically for typical configuration (e.g number of instances) of ordinary component types. The configuration has to be refined manually for more unaccustomed information.

[5] Building encompasses the generation of makefiles for checking out the last versions of components, compiling and producing executables.

- There is no overview of available components.
- No description of similarities and differences between components and component versions is available.
- It is difficult to describe dependencies between components.
- No description of how components can and should be composed, and the characteristics of the aggregates.

A basic requirement is to provide *visibility* of the overall system structure, clearly indicating which parts of the system are common and which vary. It should be possible to express that variability in one part of the system depends on the choice of variants for other items (constraints).

7.3.2 Tool Support for System Modelling

Functional modelling is done by drawing diagrams that show the different structural components and interactions between the components. Interactions are modelled through message sequence charts. As this is done in a paper form, it cannot serve as input to any tool for implementation. Maintenance is often done directly at the code level, thus leading to inconsistencies between the code and the models. Tool support at the system modelling level is highly needed.

7.3.3 Complexity of System Configuration

The system configuration is expressed in a configuration file which is parsed at system start-up by the TST run-time system. The system configuration allows one to configure the number of instances[6], the number of subinstances[7], the CPU board numbers and various other data. For example, the system configuration also covers the hardware configuration such as the configuration of radio and telephone lines. Details of the user interface, e.g. user positions, services accessible to each user and layout of each user interface, is described in the configuration file. The system configuration file contains much information and can be huge, several hundred kilobytes of text!

The configuration data are structured in records. Various configuration records can be associated to TST process and FSM entities. E.g. standard configuration records and queue description records are related to process, while data records abstract data type records are related to FSMs. The records may be associated to entity types or instances. It is possible to express default instance configurations.

The support for system configuration provided by TST is not satisfactory:

- The notation used in the configuration file is complex and extremely compact, causing problems for human decoding and comprehension.
- The configuration file is huge and difficult to maintain.

---

[6] instances is used for number of processes

[7] subinstances is used for number of FSMs

- The dependencies between configuration data are not formally described. This also leads to redundant information.
- The value domains for configuration data are not formally described.

7.3.4 Complexity of System Building

The current building system is complicated to use and relies heavily on developers detailed knowledge about the implementation and limitations of components. The configuration is time consuming and resource demanding due to its complexity.

The system building process depends on a large number of issues: hardware platform and distribution, run-time organisation of the application, non-functional requirements, and of course the contents of the actual system. Automated support which takes account of these complexities and ensure consistent choices is required.

7.3.5 Partial Configuration Binding

Garex would also be able to configure a system in several steps, thus allowing people from the development department to set detailed technical configuration parameters (e.g. hardware addresses) while people with no knowledge of the implementation (e.g. from the marketing department) could set other parameters (e.g. key positions of the user interface).

7.3.6 Evolution Support

As delivered systems evolve due to changing requirements and new system for different operating environments are created, new versions of the components are created.

Traditionally there are two types of system evolution, namely evolution over time (due to corrections, product enhancements, adaptations to new platform etc.) and evolution arising from customisations carried out for specific customers. These give rise to the number of respectively revisions and variants of components. According to the Garex' methodology, the majority of variants are represented by the system "configuration" mechanism.

Evolution over time of components and system must however be managed through other mechanisms. A version management system must provide reliable reproduction of delivered systems, handle temporary variants during development and testing etc.

7.4   The PROTEUS Approach

The PROTEUS project and the PROTEUS approach to software evolution is explained in Chapter 6.3. Garex participated as an application company in PROTEUS, using the OORAM design method.

7.4.1 OORAM with Tool Support.

The OORAM method [Ree95] and tools [TAS] provide a comprehensive environment for object oriented analysis, design and implementation in a wide range of application domains. The OORAM method and tools support life cycle stages from early requirements analysis and system architecture through final system implementation and maintenance. The OORAM tools have an open architecture permitting integration with other tools.

The methodology comprises modelling of role models with:

- role diagrams and descriptions,
- flow diagrams for messages between different roles, products or results from role models,
- information needs for different roles,
- synthesis of role models to link up related process models and determine which roles naturally fit together,

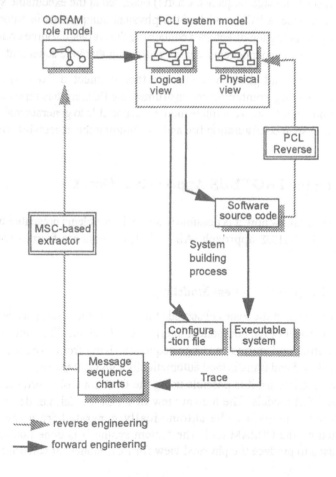

Fig. 7.2. The PROTEUS + OORAM approach

- synthesis of roles and assignment of synthesised roles to actors. By this we specify which roles a particular actor must play (one actor usually plays different roles) and his complete information needs.

A fully integrated work environment which supports the overall modelling work process for team is an integral part of OORAM. In the context of PROTEUS, an additional tool is provided, allowing generation of PCL templates from parts of an OORAM model.

7.4.2   Garex Development Process

Fig. 7.2. presents an overview of the different models and data representations at GAREX and how they are related. The details are elaborated in Section 7.5.

For existing systems parts of an initial PCL model can be produced automatically:

- A PCL model of the logical system can be automatically generated from the OO-RAM role model. This OORAM model is itself constructed semi-automatically from the traces (Message Sequence Charts) observed at the executable systems.
- Using PCL reverse, a PCL model of the physical components is automatically produced by scanning the directories containing the software source code and analysing component dependencies, e.g. by extracting #include statements.

The PCL logical and physical views are then connected. New systems are composed by selecting, combining and instrumenting PCL entities representing the reusable components. From a complete model it is possible to generate makefiles for producing the system configuration file and for building the executable system.

7.5   Using the PROTEUS Approach at Garex

In this section, we show how it is possible to solve the problems presented in Section 7.3 using the PROTEUS approach. All PCL fragments are from a real Garex application.

7.5.1   Tool Support for System Modelling

Reverse engineering of the traces observed at the executable system is used in order to construct a model of the component interfaces in OORAM. The runtime support allows generating and storing message sequence charts from executions. These charts are analysed and transformed automatically into OORAM roles.

From role descriptions, it is possible using the OORAM tool to produce process, FSM and subFSM models. The logical view of a PCL model, i.e. descriptions of individual components, can be automatically generated from the OORAM representation by the OORAM tool. The system synthesis is done manually. PCL Reverse is used to produce the physical view for PCL models of software systems.

PCL Edit/Browse allows graphical visualisation and manipulation of the complete PCL model. PCL compiler provides analysis of models for consistency and completeness. From the complete model and a particular version descriptor, the PCL Bind generates a bound PCL model which represents an unique system instance.

7.5.2 Complexity of System Configuration

The challenge was to replace a huge and complex system configuration file by a comprehensible and compact PCL model.

The PCL system model was extended with attributes describing configurable data. Some configuration information is common to all components, while other is particular to a specific components. Correspondingly, configuration data is expressed in generic (an_inst_process) or specific (i_operator) families:

```
family an_inst_process
    attributes
        // standard configuration record
        cpu_adr: integer; cpu_bck_adr: integer;
        STD_CNF := " ";
    end
end

family i_operator inherits an_inst_process
    attributes
        ...
        // used to generate configuration
        opt_1 := " "; opt_2 := " ";
        STD_CNF := "," ++ opt_1 ++ "," ++ opt_2;
    end
```

Similarly to attributes controlling the system variability, the configuration attributes are bound in a version descriptor:

```
version v_i_operator of i_operator
    attributes
        cpu_adr := 255; cpu_bck_adr := 254;
        opt_1 := "blue"; opt_2 := "french";
    end
end
```

The configuration of multiple instances of run-time components is also supported by PCL. The numbers of instance and the configuration of these instances are specified in the version descriptors.

In order to produce configuration records from the configuration attributes, PCL tool entities are defined. The PCL *tool* construct allows declarative specifications of the steps in the building process by defining the signature and behaviours of software tools. Here the building consists of the generation of the configuration file, not the generation of the executable file. For producing a process configuration record the tool `tool_process_std_cfg` is defined:

```
tool tool_process_std_cfg
    attributes
        cpu_adr:integer; cpu_bck_adr:integer;
        STD_CNF;
        XX := "\\n\\t#S," ++ cpu_adr ++ ","
            ++ cpu_bck_adr ++ STD_CNF;
    end
// No inputs
    outputs out => pr_std_cfg; end
    scripts
        build := echo ++" \""++ XX ++"\" > "++ out;
    end
end
```

The build script specifies the actual command line for tool invocation. The output section specifies that a file classified "pr_std_cfg" is generated. Such a file is associated to the generic family "an_inst_process":

```
family an_inst_process
    ...
    physical
        // standard configuration record
        std => (classification type := pr_std_cfg,
            classification status := derived);
    end
end
```

Several tools and classifications are modelled for producing the different kinds of configuration records. Tools are specified for concatenating these records into one configuration file. From the PCL model annotated with configuration attributes and configuration tools descriptions, the PCL tool set can produce a makefile containing derivation rules for generating an appropriate TST configuration file.

7.5.3   Complexity of System Building

For modelling system building processes, software tools used in the conventional system building process can be described in the same model using the *tool* construct.

Complex derivation steps, far exceeding the capabilities of e.g. Make [FEL79], can be declaratively defined. A C compiler may be modelled as:

```
tool cc
    attributes
        CC: string default "cc ";
```

```
        CFLAGS: string default " ";
     CINCL: string default " ";
     end
     inputs in => c-source; end
     outputs out => obj-code; end
     scripts
         build := CC ++ CFLAGS ++ CINCL ++ "-o "
                  ++ out ++ " -c " ++ in;
         depend:= ...
     end
 end
```

Tool options or switches are denoted by PCL attributes. These attributes can be assigned generally for all components:

```
family a__physical_process
   attributes
         // compilation include path
         CINCL := "-I " ++ `work_top ++ "common/ ";
```

or set for all files associated to a specific family:

```
   family oplorstdss inherits a_physical_process
      attributes
          CINCL := "-I " ++ `work_top ++ "comm_op/ ";
```

or for an individual file:

```
   family oplorstdss inherits a_physical_process
      physical
          ...
          p3 => "audio_r.c" (CINCL := audio_inc_path);
      end
   end
```

The complete model is processed by the PCL Makegen and makefiles produced. Dependency rules are automatically generated, either derived from source files by means of depend scripts (to extract e.g. #include dependencies between C files), or due to explicitly declared dependency relationships in the PCL model.

7.5.4 Partial Configuration Binding

The PCL tool set supports partial binding of system models, enabling a limited form of partial specification and incremental completion of detail mentioned in [BIG87]. If a version descriptor is incomplete, i.e. if values for some attributes are missing, a partially bound family will result from binding. This corresponds to a limited set of possible systems. A partially bound model can be further bound at some later stage, resolving the remaining ambiguity.

7.5.5   Evolution Support

To handle the problem of file versions, we have chosen a two-tier repository approach. The contents and the descriptions of file versions are managed by a special tool called the Repository. PCL supports intensional version selection, controlled through the PCL system model.

The PCL model is extended in order to support selection of versions of files from a the Repository. Selecting versions of files based on annotations is easily done by associating *exported* attributes to entities in the model. The version selection attributes are bound in the same way as other attributes by means of a version descriptor:

```
family a__physical_process
    attributes

        ...
        // selection from repository
        customer exported;
    end
version v_i_operator of i_operator
    attributes

        ...
        customer := "Schiphol";
    end
end
```

Version selection is usually applied after the bind operation, and allows generation of makefiles with automatic check-out rules.

Selecting the latest versions of files or selecting versions based on explicit version number can also be done easily using the exported attributes *time* or *repository_version*.

7.6   Evaluation

A subset of the components of GAREX 210 were selected in order to evaluate PROTEUS technology [FLO95]. Using this component subset, it is possible to generate several systems which have previously been delivered to customers. The evaluation focuses on the generation of the system configuration file.

The selected application is quite huge (almost 500 000 lines of code and 10 000 lines of configuration data) as shown in Table 7.1.

PCL models were developed which provide good overall system visibility. Separate models for system building and system configuration were produced. The models describe all system variability in a single formalism, structural differences, varying associated physical objects, component version selection, tool processing for system building, configuration parameters (and the value domain), and tools for configuration generation. From this unified model consistent component selection, system building and configuration is ensured by automated tools.

Table 7.1. Component Size

Component type	Number of components	Number of files	Code size (lines)
process	13	58	29 200
FSM	73	368	403 154
subFSM	9	41	16 617
TOTAL	95	467	448 971
Configuration		1	10 000

The models include the description of processes, FSMs and subFSMs. ADOs, the common definitions and the run-time platform (TST) are modelled as external libraries components. Including detailed information about ADOs and TST was experimented in another company (see Chapter 6).

The size of the PCL model for system building is shown in Table 7.2.. In this table, we distinguish between:

- a standard model, i.e. shipped with the PCL tools,
- the generic entities,
- the entities automatically produced by PCL reverse,
- the entities manually produced,
- the version descriptors.

The size of the generated makefile is about 6000 lines while the PCL model is about 4000 lines. No significant size reduction is obtained, but it is important to remember that the same PCL model can be used to generate various system instances. The PCL model contains more information than the makefile, as it describes system structural variability, version selection of associated physical objects, differences in processing tool parameters etc.

The size of the PCL model for configuration generation is shown in Table 7.3.. The version descriptors are large due to incomplete implementation of the PCL toolset. We believe that their sizes can be reduced to 10% of the current sizes (that is about 160 lines for the example shown in the table). A major benefit of using PCL is the consistency of the configuration information: dependencies can easily be described in PCL but not in the configuration files. Another significant benefit is the improved maintainability due to the good readability of the PCL models.

The main conclusions for the evaluation are:

Table 7.2. Size of the PCL Model for System Building

PCL model	Number of PCL entities	PCL code size (lines)
standard	81	556
generic	11	140
automatically prod.	98	1279
manually written	177	1878
version descriptor	3	48
TOTAL	370	3901
Makefile		5995

Table 7.3. Size of the PCL Model for Configuration Generation

PCL model	Numb. of PCL entities/ configuration records	code size (lines)
PCL		
generic	42	524
application	152	2074
version descriptor	38	1619
Configuration file	80	80

- Using PCL reverse, it is easy to produce an initial system model from an existing application.
- The initial system model is rapidly extended with variability and building information. The generation of makefiles for building a system instance is a powerful feature.
- The system configuration can be expressed at a higher level of abstraction than it is done in TST configuration file. The resulting model of the configuration parameters is easy to read and understand. The dependencies between configuration parameters can be expressed. The version descriptors are too voluminous, but this problem will be solved when the tool implementation will support the complete notation for multiple instances.
- The implementation of interactive binding is not satisfactory. Especially, there is no mechanism to automatically update the version descriptor i.e. store assignments made interactively.
- Using the repository enables one to easily express in a PCL model (or version descriptor) which components are to be selected. The components can also be annotated using Repository Browser, thus allowing a delivered version to be easily se-

lected from the PCL toolset, without giving version numbers for each individual source file.

- RCS is a primitive and not very user-friendly tool. Repository Browser provides the user with a complete overview of the versions and version groups, and with advanced functions for version management:
- The intentional version selection mechanism is easy to use but it is quite limited. It is not possible to associate priorities to the selection criteria.

8 Bull

- **Consultant Company:** Bull REBOOT team
- **Size of involved team:**
- **Domain:** Workflow support
- **Reuse experience:** some
- **Size of application:**
- **Programming language:**
- **Type of software:** Interactive sw tools
- **Scope:** horizontal
- **Granularity:** Large components
- **Technology:** REBOOT

8.1 Introduction

This experience has been carried out at Bull S.A. in producing software for client server based solutions in the office systems marketplace.

The activities of the division divides into development of application specific products (e.g. for image processing) and platform related products (e.g. for user interface).

The major motivator for examining the benefit of reuse has been the need for combating increased competition in an ever growing client-server market. This market is typified by high volume software suppliers, an increasing number of small specialist suppliers and a fast rate of change across the typical range of products available to the market.

We will explain how reuse has helped Bull work more efficiently in this changing marketplace.

8.2 Preparation

Initial analysis revealed a good potential for reuse in the division. This view was based on:

- the coexistence of several product streams and several sub-system development streams;

- recognition of the need to deal with a high rate of change in the operating and development systems;
- recognition of the immediate benefit of rationalizing the organisational structure to configure products from common sub-systems – thus releasing more resources to product improvement;
- recognition of the potential of the resulting organisation to evolve a reusable component base to be used in product development.

The primary goal was to improve time to market for functional and platform changes. Reconfigurable products would be constructed to meet market requirements from a base of reusable components. Improvement would be in flexibility and quality of products, with increased overall productivity.

Workflow systems were chosen as a pilot domain because this field is dependent upon, and builds on, many innovative and emerging technologies. The strategy was first to pilot the introduction of reuse to workflow systems development while involving the image and document processing teams. Then, the resulting reuse technology would be deployed to the entire department, and later, more generally within the company.

8.3   Results

8.3.1   What has been Achieved

The organisation has been transformed to a way of working in which:

- more resources are allocated to meet the functional requirements of the application domain;
- there is a greater awareness of the need for, and the availability of quality components which can be built into quality products;
- the emphasis is to configure products from a growing base of reusable components; and
- additions to the component base are developed or acquired to meet the identified product requirements of those domains to which the division supplies products.

The effect is a re-balancing between the product and component base to supply competitive solutions across the overall marketplace, specializing these to the needs of the marketplace and building up the component base as a value added program.

8.3.2   The Stage of Transformation Achieved

The view within the division is that the foundation has been laid to really begin to reap benefit from this approach. There is always a need for achieving some degree of critical mass, to arrive at a turning point, after which the major gains begin to be made. In this example, the division:

- has refocused to exploit reuse,
- identifies, develops, and reuses more common sub-systems,
- is growing a component base.

8.3.3   The Cost of Transformation

The evidence shows little difference in cost between developing software FOR reuse compared with traditional software development. Consistent use of the REBOOT methodology results in the transformation costs being absorbed in the on-going development programs. Well-planned reuse actions enabled to both institutionalise and control reuse. As a result, the additional costs have been recovered within the development of the first version.

8.3.4   Benefits

The organisation has achieved a balance between product and component development and, as a result, evolves the products and the components in a consistent manner. Significantly less effort is needed for implementation detail and basic technology development. The combined effect of dedicating more effort to providing required product features, and of the availability of suitable components to meet these requirements, is an improved response to market need.

In addition, the organisation has become more focused on configuring products from proven parts and has started to integrate products into other environments.

The overall benefit of this has been to position the company to offer more competitive products supplied in a shorter time. For example, the new version of the flowPATH product offers much more functionality which mostly comes from reuse of large components (e.g. ImageEditor, Communication layer, ContentPATH). Moreover, other teams in the division as well as product line people have become converted and reuse-minded too. As a result, the overall product line is getting more consistent, compatible and attractive.

8.3.5   Typical Experienced Cost Benefits

In this committed and organised reuse program, experience includes:

- a sub-system, with a development cost of 4 PY (Person-Years), reused 5 times, saving 20 PY;
- a sub-system, with a development cost of 2 PY, reused twice, saving 4 PY;
- a framework, with a development cost of 2.5 PY, reused twice, saving 2 PY each time;
- a stand-alone product whose parts have been reused in another product, saving 0.5 PY;
- a generator, with a development cost of 2 PY, expected to save 4 PY.

The extra-cost for developing these reusable sub-systems and frameworks is about 30% of the normal development cost while costs of reuse are quite low (1-4 Person-Months) compared to the savings.

These benefits continue to grow as the number of projects reusing these well-designed and well-tested frameworks and sub-systems increases.

Last but not least, savings in maintenance are also substantial because the shared sub-systems are preserved as a single code base, thus keeping the support costs down to a fraction of what they would be if separate groups had to maintain their specific source code separately.

8.3.6 Lessons learned

Among the lessons learned are:

- Reuse in-the-large (reuse of sub-systems) yields more benefits than reuse in-the-small.
- Development FOR reuse, coordinated with the development of application specific products, has had a beneficial impact on the architecture: it naturally leads to a clearer abstraction of the developed (sub)system that better supports late changes in requirements. Thus development FOR reuse adds to the quality of the developed application right from the start.
- Developing WITH reuse clearly motivates people to develop new reusable components.
- Market and return on investment must be carefully studied and followed-up. Since the technology is evolving rapidly, some components may become rapidly obsolete.

8.3.7 Experience with the REBOOT Methodology

This example indicates how the extent of such a transformation requires a complete methodology that addresses organisation, management, engineering and technology. Planning involved defining a start point from a realistic and accurate view of the organisation and the way in which it operated at the time, and then defining programs as a series of manageable, evolutionary steps. Planning guidelines were derived from the methodology and customised to the domain of application by the REBOOT consultants.

In short, the methodology was applied in the following way:

- The organisation was judged to be ready for reuse, characterised by several vertical product streams supported by several horizontal development teams.
- The organisation was prepared for reuse before deploying the technology through established engineering approaches.
- Assessments showed a satisfactory maturity level, as measured in a reuse capability maturity model.
- Component development programs to grow the base of reusable components are funded from product development programs.

- Market analysis, involving the product marketing managers, has been established to guide the further development of the component base.
- The evolution was planned and conducted in manageable steps, monitoring results achieved against outlay of effort and resource. Goals and measures were set and assessed against the measures in the reuse maturity model.

9 SIA

- **Consultant Company:**   TXT
- **Size of involved team:**   8
- **Domain:**   avionics
- **Reuse experience:**   some
- **Size of application:**   70,000 LOC
- **Programming language:**   ADA
- **Type of software:**   software system
- **Scope:**   horizontal
- **Granularity:**   fine grained
- **Technology:**   REBOOT

9.1   Introduction

SIA is a system engineering company concerned with electronic equipment for flight and ground applications (aircraft, spacecraft, industrial, etc.)

The software development department designs and develops real-time software systems for both ground and flight applications, following military and/or international standards.

Reuse of software components mainly at design and coding level was considered at the beginning of the experiment a key point to improve the production process. In fact, in spite of the relatively high maturity level achieved by the company, with respect to the CMM[1], there was an unexploited potential for reuse that was expected to provide a major increase to SIA's competitiveness.

The application involved in the experiment was represented by a family of test integration systems for electronic equipment, named AIDASS (Advanced Integrated Data Acquisition and Simulation/Stimulation), that was originally developed for Aerospace projects.

AIDASS supports the hardware/software integration and test of electronic equipment, sub-systems and complete systems. The integration and test activities

---

[1] Capability Maturity Model, model for the assessment of software process maturity developed at the Software Engineering Institute, Carnegie Mellon University, USA.

are carried on by connecting the AIDASS to the electronic units and by performing real-time data acquisition, simulation and stimulation. Real time environment simulation can be performed by software modules to be integrated by the user with the AIDASS core, that provides an appropriate standard interface and software utilities. During the execution of the integration and test campaign it is also possible to stimulate the electronic equipment and to perform failure simulation. The application provides a textual and graphical post-run analysis utility. It performs an in-depth evaluation and reporting of test results on a predefined set of data recorded in real-time mode.

SIA is the major developer of AIDASS system, it is responsible for its maintenance and for its subsequent updates according to evolving requirements.

The reuse introduction pilot project focused mainly on the software development aspects in order to identify new reusable components or to re-engineer them starting from the previous implementation.

This activity mainly encompassed low level design and implementation issues.

Before starting the pilot, people at SIA were concerned about three main issues:

- safety issues had not traditionally been addressed when dealing with reuse strategies with the risky consequence that software reuse might have a negative impact on systems safety;
- reuse methodology from research was seen as having had a very low degree of industrial penetration and impact on the industrial software engineering practice. The known industrial reuse methods were seen as not directly applicable to the general audience;
- changes in the organisational aspects were seen as having potential for introducing conflicts among persons and difficulties in using the equipment.

Working together with TXT, SIA was able to clarify the initial doubts and related uncertainties.

9.2   Motivation for Reuse

An initial analysis of the general status at SIA enabled to detect the major weaknesses of the development process. Reuse specific metrics to extract quality parameters about code and design were also deemed necessary so as to assess the produced reusable software.

Even if the pilot project was concerned with AIDASS, the variety of the applications developed at SIA, from satellite control systems to simulators such as AIDASS, suggested an horizontal approach to reuse as the best suited one to start with: aiming at producing general purpose components to be reused across the entire application domain was therefore the initial objective of the pilot project.Further experience with reuse could then lead to identify coarser grained reusable components, but this was not considered to be an objective of the pilot.

9.3   Reuse Experiences and Opportunities

As mentioned before analysis of the initial status at SIA was carried out based on the Reuse Maturity Model defined by REBOOT.

Since SIA already had previous experience with reuse, the analysis was centred around a critical evaluation of the reuse specific activities included in the software development life-cycle and on their actual integration in the life-cycle itself.

The software development life-cycle model was highly influenced by the specific domain of the applications developed at SIA. In fact, most of the software developed in this company is software for avionic systems and the company has to follow the guidelines imposed by its customers.

The activities carried out at SIA start with the acquisition of the system requirements from the customers (aerospace companies). Analysis and design of the system are then performed. In particular, the design phase is carried out making use of HOOD methodology and tools.

The reuse program was at an experimental stage and it was centred around the definition of an in house reusable software database and the appointment of a Reuse Manager in charge of maintaining the database, "promoting" reuse of stored components and acting as inter project liaison.

The reusable database contained 7 components and 3 sub-systems. Together with software compilation units and configuration information were maintained.

The basic reuse process enforced at SIA at the beginning of the pilot is briefly described in the following.

As shown in the picture, reuse oriented activities were carried out in an orthogonal way with respect to the software development life-cycle. In other words, no major change was performed in the development process model, but rather, additional "parallel" activities were defined.

The model was conceived in such a way that its application is rather simple and aims at impacting as little as possible the standard life-cycle model within the company. In particular, the activities performed as part of the evaluation of developed software (arrow 1) and the analysis of the application so as to extract potentially reusable aspects of the system under development (arrow 3) were performed in an unmanaged and unstructured way and were once more based on personal experience and common-sense.

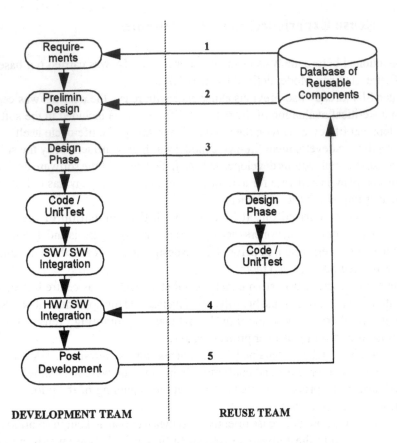

Fig. 9.1. Basic Reuse Process at SIA. The arrows are to be read as follows:
arrow 1: retrieve from reusable components database any reusable feature coming from previous experiences, including requirements of the systems, not necessarily expressed by customers;
arrow 2: reuse components from the database (design WITH reuse);
arrow 3: focus on potentially reusable aspects of the application (design FOR reuse);
arrow 4: re-introduce components developed for reuse in the normal life-cycle and test them in the real application context;
arrow 5: add to reuse asset after performing a post-development analysis.

The major criticism to the initial implementation of the reuse process is that the definition of reusable components, their reuse in other projects, their insertion in a repository, the repository maintenance as well as the publication and the distribution of description catalogues is still a handicraft and the type of services which may be offered is therefore neither formalised nor controlled. However, the experience was a positive one and considered suitable to be improved with the introduction of more sophisticated working methodologies.

9.4   Target Reuse Organisation

The reuse programme at SIA was geared to improve SIA's reuse state-of-practice. The starting point of the project was that of detecting the main deficiencies of the organisation as far as the reuse enactment program already in use was concerned. Main areas of possible improvements were then identified based on the REBOOT Maturity Model and they were compared with the specific company objectives. The result of this process was the identification of four main goals for the remaining part of the pilot projects:

- *Metrics:* Analysis and definition of significant metrics for the qualification of software components were deemed absolutely necessary for the enactment of reuse in a highly safety-sensitive environment.
- *Classification:* Classification structures and supporting mechanisms were seen as a first step towards the facilitation of components retrieval;
- *Reusable components repository consolidation and enhancement:* This was judged an indispensable means for the management of a larger number of components.
- *Reusable components repository population:* The real test for reuse would only come when the components would be produced and put to work.

9.5   Major Changes Needed

From the methodological point of view, the project focused mainly on the identification of reusable components starting from existing software applications.

Re-engineering techniques, applied in the design and coding phases of the software life-cycle, were deemed suitable to improve the organisation capabilities in maintaining developed applications.

As far as CMM is concerned SIA was evaluated as being at level 4, indication a very high level of process refinement and potential. On the other hand, its reuse maturity was on the average no higher than level 2, and in many areas as low as level 1.

The purpose of the first phase of the experiment was that of consolidating the organisation's reuse practices; that is, consolidate level 2. The main steps that need to be taken towards this goal are described in the following.

The analysis of the assessment results highlighted the following changes needed to improve reuse practice in SIA.

From the *organisational* point of view, the reuse programme was extended to more than one project and the process model changed accordingly. Furthermore, the organisation management allocated the resources necessary to enact the reuse strategy and followed up the reuse plan.

These objectives were defined at the beginning of the pilot with the intention of reconsidering them at the end of the pilot and comparing their feasibility with the results obtained.

From the *project management* point of view, metrics were deemed essential for the evaluation of the effort spent in reuse related activities. In order to make the measurement process easier, suitable forms, possibly complying with the organisations standards were foreseen.

Finally, the major effort was devoted to two major activities: component library enhancement and development process refinement. As far as the development process related activities are concerned, the focus was on the re-engineering of potentially reusable components.

The main focus, as far as metrics related activities are concerned, was on product quality/reuse metrics which were chosen among those automatically computed by available tools. On the other hand, process quality metrics were computed by hand mainly taking into account the effort spent during the development.

9.6   Summary of Experiment Results

The quantitative results of the pilot were quite encouraging. First of all the assessment of the company reuse maturity performed at the beginning of the project indicated that the company reuse strategy was overall an ad hoc procedure (level 1 of the REBOOT Reuse Maturity Model) mainly based on the capabilities and the skills of the single individuals even if the basis for a more structured way of working had been put.

At the end of the experiment the company had shifted to a more systematic reuse strategy with a higher level of commitment from the management and a set of guidelines to support the developers in their activities (i.e. at level 2).

The pilot project had an overall duration of 18 months including the initial assessment phase and it involved a growing number of people: from 2 people initially allocated to the project, the team grew to incorporate 8 members.

The start-up training of the project team lasted 5 days, spanning from the presentation of basic concepts to more sophisticated reuse notions. Specific attention was also paid to the development of reusable components in Ada (the programming language most widely spread within the organisation).

Once the conditions for starting the experiment were achieved, the actual process of analysing existing software with the intention of extracting reusable components started and SIA was coached by TXT Ingegneria Informatica. The coaching involved 8 to 10 man/days for the first six months of the experiment and 4 man days for the following six months.

The development activities carried out in the "FOR reuse" phase lead to the definition of 40 potentially reusable components - to be compared with the 7 components available before the experiment.

The development of the new software system, starting from the identified components - the so called development WITH reuse activities - lead to a percentage of savings equal to 20%.

Overall, and besides the quantitative results just presented, the pilot project carried out at SIA was quite successful from several points of view and impacted the organisation at different levels.

The objectives set at the beginning of the experiment were not only achieved, but even surpassed.

The approach taken since the beginning of the experiment was a pragmatic one, aiming at the definition of real-world, useful indications especially tailored on the needs of the specific application domain. In line with this expectations, guidelines for the development of reusable components - that is for supporting developers in their activities "FOR reuse" - were identified together with guidelines for the development of new applications from reusable components, that is, to be used during the "development WITH reuse" phase of the reusable software development life-cycle.

Essential aides for the management of reusable software components were also implemented in a prototypical form: a prototype repository was set up, a component model and a components classification schema especially tailored on the application domain were defined.

A good level of reuse culture dissemination within the organisation was achieved during the pilot project by means of the training of the development team members, the involvement of selected development team members in the experiment and by increasing the sensitiveness of the management.

The pilot project was also crucial in the identification of future areas of improvement.

A corporate-wide programme for the realisation of a census of the companies assets was launched. In particular, based on the pieces of component-related information that were identified and deemed significant within the pilot project a component profile was defined to be filled in by the different departments in the companies of the corporate.

Furthermore, a new project was also launched which starting from EUROWARE technology is aimed at setting up a corporate wide repository for the classification, qualification, storage, search and retrieval of software assets.

An interesting observation of the experiment carried out at SIA is the reiterate observation of how reuse is not a natural consequence of a highly sophisticated software development process as it is perceived by the Capability Maturity Model and that special care must be paid in terms of organisational structure and resource allocation to deploy reuse in a software producing company.

Progress in this direction has been made and, besides REBOOT and its Reuse Maturity Model, a comprehensive approach is taken also by Caper Jones in his "Assessment and Control of Software Risks" [Jon94] where the failure by the software industry to have developed generic designs or models, is seen as a severe problem associated with low productivity, low quality, long schedules, excessive time to market, and high maintenance costs.

10 Instrumentation Laboratory

- **Consultant Company:** TXT
- **Size of involved team:** medium
- **Domain:** health care instruments
- **Reuse experience:** small
- **Type of software:** embedded
- **Scope:** single product-line
- **Granularity:** domain specific interpreters/O-O frameworks
- **Technology:** REBOOT

10.1 Introduction

Instrumentation Laboratory is a company that builds critical health-care instruments (blood analysis and electrolyte).

The type of applications developed by IL is represented by complex medical machines corresponding to complex software systems and embedded applications. In particular, the systems usually consist of

- three to four processors
- embedded software
- data management software
- communication software (protocols)
- user interface (CUI and GUI)

10.2 Motivation for Reuse

The initial analysis carried out at IL pointed out that the core of the activities consisted in porting on different hardware and software platforms the existing products so as to improve maintainability and to add features and new parameters. In particular, the expected improvement in passing from the old version to the new one was that of enhancing the functionalities to phase them with new customer requirements.

Furthermore IL was interested in reusing requirements specification from previous projects and to build "blocks" for future reuse.

In this scenario, the main interest concerning reuse was therefore centred around domain analysis and reuse of existing subsystems.

10.3 Opportunities

In order to acquire and maintain a leading edge over competitors, the company objective was that of significantly reducing the time to market of new apparatuses.

In particular, the company was interested in achieving a reduction of the effort required for each project from 20-30 person/years to less than 20 p/y, and a reduction of the time to market from 2-3 years to 1 year.

The relatively long time span between the definition of new requirements and the release of a new apparatus was partially due to the critical nature of the systems developed. Special care had to be devoted to Verification and Validation activities as well as to Quality Assurance activities in general. The compliance to quality standards was, in this specific domain, of particular relevance.

10.4 Experiences

At the beginning of the experiment IL software applications were already developed following a common architecture which allowed a certain degree of reuse. This common architecture consisted of:

- Hardware platform
- Firmware
- Intermediate layer 1: interpreters of high level languages for the definition of abstract machines
- Intermediate layer 2: interpreters between basic arithmetic libraries and the interface with the operator of the medical device.

The structure of the interpreters is such that they can often be reused in different contexts (i.e. for the development of applications for different devices of the same line)

The reuse enacted at IL though was still not reflected by the organisational structure. Furthermore, even if it was explicitly part of the process model used to develop the applications the actual reuse of portions of existing systems was performed based on personal knowledge and experience.

10.5 Target Organisation

Even though the organisation showed a rather high quality level both in the process model adopted and followed, and in the checking of the product quality performed, there existed several areas for improvement when it came to reuse-related issues.

The first goal was that of improving the organisational structure since, even if reuse activities were already considered and integrated in the development life-cycle, reuse was not actually enacted to its full potential.

In parallel with the organisational restructuring further areas of reuse needed to be found, possibly defining application frameworks which were to build upon the basis of the initially used system architecture.

10.6 Major Changes Needed

The scenario depicted up to now enables to identify a large potential for the introduction of a reuse programme in different directions. In particular, three possible areas of concern have been identified; they are represented by

- concepts and algorithms reuse: blood analysis methodologies and procedures are a company asset and very often are patented by the company;
- code reuse
- test cases reuse
- requirements specification reuse
- reuse of architectures

Great benefits are also expected in carrying out a thorough analysis of domain specific characteristics so as to maximise reuse opportunities and, possibly identify new reusable items besides the ones mentioned above.

Finally, IL is considering to introduce C++ as a programming language. Even if the switch to an object oriented approach to software development has not been defined at the time of writing, this potentially increases the chances of obtaining reusable components.

10.7 Summary of Experiment Results

Even if the experiment had not reached its peak at the time of writing of this book, the experience is summarised in this chapter because it is a very significant example of the damages that the failure of a reuse program can cause within an organisation regardless of the software engineering culture level and of the maturity of the process within the organisation itself.

In fact, an attempt had already been made in the past to introduce reuse at IL, but it had failed. Drawing from this previous experience and with the support of the approach proposed by the REBOOT methodology, a different reuse introduction program was defined.

The analysis carried out at the beginning of the experiment at IL lead to the identification of suitable candidate projects to experiment with reuse in a "new" way. The main requirement for the reintroduction program was that it needed to be performed in a step by step way and that reuse was performed on a project by project basis.

This was not considered to hinder reuse enactment in IL given the company's product strategy whereby each product was released in many different subsequent versions. Furthermore, the considerable size of the projects carried out at IL and their time span also played a favourable role in the deployment of reuse. The strong technical background of project mangers as well as the commitment they showed towards the new technology were also considered to be a plus.

The reuse introduction program, though, suffered from the negative influence of what was seen by a portion of the management as a negative experience with reuse.

Project managers and middle management had therefore to struggle to find a way around this problem promoting reuse within their teams and advertising results at upper management levels.

For this reason, as well as for the considerable maturity and capability of the company (with respect to CMM), metrication of the reuse process was taken into particular account.

11 BPM

- **Consultant Company:** TXT
- **Size of involved team:** 25
- **Domain:** banking
- **Reuse experience:** small
- **Size of application:** 100,000 statements
- **Programming language:** COBOL 2
- **Type of software:** data intensive software system
- **Scope:** product line, emphasis on application domain
- **Granularity:** fine grained
- **Technology:** REBOOT

11.1 Introduction

BPM is an Italian bank present all over the country.

As in many other cases, it was suggested and decided to introduce reuse in a step by step fashion starting with the experimentation of the REBOOT methodology on a pilot project. The chosen application dealt with investment policies in the field of life insurance policies supporting the sale of insurance products within bank agencies.

The development of this application was considered as a first step in the introduction of a reuse-oriented approach to software development. The results yielded by the selected experimental application should, in fact, be regarded as the basis for the definition of a reuse introduction programme impacting strategic areas of the software development department at BPM.

At the end of the SER project, the reuse introduction program at BPM was lagging behind and had not achieved the expected results due partially to a large-scale reorganisation within the company and partially to an inappropriate selection of the pilot project. The report concerning the experience at BPM, nevertheless, is included in this book because the initial steps in the program represent a good sample of a different application domain. Furthermore, it is interesting to observe how part of the delay in the deployment of the program could have been avoided by choosing a different pilot.

11.2   Motivation for Reuse

The experiment started at BPM stemmed from the need for reducing the time-to-market of banking products. The enactment of a reuse policy was felt as a promising means for the reduction of the time and effort necessary to develop software applications supporting new banking products as well as for enhancing the quality of the applications themselves in terms of reliability, security and performance. This reduction was not expected to be a short term effect of one experiment, but was seen more as a result to be achieved in the long run.

The need for the available information to be used in a more effective way was felt as more and more crucial at BPM. This overall objective was also associated with the growing amount of data that are to be processed by the applications developed by BPM and to the increasing demand for higher performance and reduced response time of the whole company information system.

In line with these objectives, the product developed in the selected pilot application was considered to be highly strategic given the necessity of BPM to provide a service that was already offered by competitors. Being able to implement the automatic support for this service in the smallest time span possible was therefore of the utmost relevance.

The idea underpinning such an experiment was that of exploiting the methodological and technological support provided as a result of the REBOOT project.

The feasibility of deploying EUROWARE was also considered: in particular, it depended upon the results obtained during the application experiment as well as on the actual feasibility and cost-effectiveness of implementing the concepts defined by EUROWARE in the development environment used at BPM at the time which was based on Lotus Notes.

During this pilot application, the technical goal was to identify the areas with highest reuse potential in the same sub-domain of the selected application and to build a pool of easily reusable components for the same subdomain.

The long term objective was that of extending the same policy to a wider range of applications.

BPM experimental application therefore focused on domain analysis issues, i.e. on how to apply and improve current object oriented domain analysis and reuse techniques in a banking domain. This involved identification and modelling of components, building a repository of reusable components, and technology transfer in the software development department.

11.3 Opportunities

The scenario that characterised BPM at the beginning of the experiment, not unlike that of many other banks world wide, was such that the acquisition of new business could be achieved by directly luring it away from its competitors.

The time-to-market for the automatic support to new banking products was expected to drop.

The desirable percentage of savings in terms of time necessary to develop a new application was around 40%.

Software quality, especially as far as reliability, performance and uniformity of the HCI across different applications, was also expected to improve.

11.4 Experiences

Before the start of the pilot experiment, reuse was taken into account to some extent, especially for the presentation aspect of the applications. In fact, the uniformity of the user interface across different application is considered to be of high priority in order to guarantee a certain level of user friendliness to the end users. Nevertheless, even for such components, the reuse process was *ad hoc* and no *formal* procedure explicitly governed the process leading to the selection of already existing HCI components so as that they could be used in the best possible way and in the best possible context.

Starting from the way of working at BPM at the time of the experiment, potential for reuse was identified in at least two different strategic areas.

The first one was oriented towards the improvement of the reuse currently practised. In particular, the definition of a procedure regulating the reuse process could have helped maximising actual reuse of HCI components.

The second one was in the direction of an optimisation of the initial practice so as to increase the potential for reuse. This particular investigation area required a thorough analysis of the domain (existing and foreseen applications in the specific sub-domain of the so called *back office consulting services*) and the definition of a plan for the reasoned introduction of reuse, including a careful evaluation of the impact that the enactment of such a plan could have on the organisation and on the development process.

Finally, previous experiments in the field of reuse was a sign of the recognised need for an improvement in this development area. Nevertheless, a real reuse culture at the organisational level was still missing and needed to be addressed so as to make a reuse program as effective as possible.

11.5 Target Organisation

The achievement of company wide fine grained reuse was the first target set for the organisation. This would also enable a consistent spread of the reuse culture and set the basis for more complex forms of reuse.

11.6 Major Changes Needed

At the organisational level more attention towards reuse matters needed to be paid by management and enforcement of reuse needed to be set as a strategically relevant objective.

At the project management level an inter project management effort had to be made so as to allow the analysis of the variability of requirements across applications and to identify common needs.

At the development process level specific activities for the development of reusable components and for their use in new applications needed to be defined.

As far as the component library is concerned, the definition of a component model was deemed necessary together with the implementation of a repository to store and manage the developed components and a component management procedure definition.

The collection of relevant data was also a change with the respect to the initial situation where no data was collected at all, especially as far as reuse related activities were concerned.

Training of the personnel involved in the experiment was considered to be the first step towards an increased sensitivity about reuse related issues and concerns.

11.7 Overall Plan

The overall plan to carry out the reuse experiment at BPM was divided into two phases. The first phase was concerned with start up related activities and FOR reuse activities and the second phase was concerned with WITH reuse activities. In particular, the following tasks were defined as making up the first phase of the experiment:

- Completion of thorough assessment using the REBOOT RMM for the identification of areas of improvement especially at the organisational level
- Training and technology transfer to enhance the reuse culture within the S/W development department
- Domain analysis based on the thorough understanding of existing applications and on the expected changes required of the application yet to be developed
- Identification, modelling and definition of potentially reusable components

- Development of a repository of reusable component based on a simple, preliminary classification schema
- Population of the repository with the identified components

The second phase of the experiment consisted in guiding the development of new applications WITH reuse. In order for this second phase to take place, the identification of specific applications in the same sub-domain needed to be carried out.

Also, further training in the area of development WITH reuse was thought to be required in order to make the experiment more effective

11.8   Experiment Objectives

A real *reuse strategy* was missing at the beginning of the experiment therefore, the main objective was that of defining a short term reuse strategy on the basis of the results of the pilot application. Such a strategy was supposed to impact a limited number of applications within the department and to focus around the validation of the results achieved during the pilot application project especially in terms of suitability of the models, procedures and techniques defined and proposed.

The requirements for such a strategy to be defined, were mainly related to the need for an understanding of the technical and organisational aspects of reuse by the management.

As far as *reuse assessment* is concerned, reuse goals needed to be defined and resources allocated by the management as part of the regular planning activities. A specific follow up for reuse related activities needed to be performed against the original plans.

Within the scope of the pilot project, draft procedures and models for assessing reuse activities needed to be proposed, tried out and validated for suitability.

A first "a posteriori" evaluation of the impact of reuse activities on the *price of the products* was scheduled based on the data collected during the pilot. The evaluation was meant to represent the basis for future "a priori" evaluations which will be constantly verified against the initial estimates so as to refine the estimate model with time.

An effort needed to be made during the pilot so as to compare the requirements of the application under development with the requirements of some other project developed or to be developed within the department (*long-term product strategy*). This comparison was in line with the overall objective of identifying new potential areas of reuse within the company.

According to the REBOOT approach four main types of dependencies between projects are established whenever a reuse oriented approach to *project management* has been chosen.

In the following the objectives of the pilot at BPM are defined for each of the different kinds of relationship.

- Management of the requirements for the project:
  high level requirements for the application to be developed within this project had already been collected without keeping reuse in due account. Further attention needed therefore be paid to the variability of requirements in the short term strategical evolution of the product line.
- Coordination with the other projects that produce reusable components that are going to be used in the project:
  a thorough domain analysis was needed. This kind of relationship was therefore strategical within the project and needed particular attention.
- Coordination with people that have developed the reusable components:
  this kind of relationship was verified and left for future analysis.
- Co-ordination with the reusable components repository manager for the acceptance of the reusable components developed in the project:
  an "ad interim" repository manager needed to be nominated within the developers team. The relationships occurring between him/her and the rest of the developers needed to be monitored so as to identify critical points for future improvement.

The main objective as far as project planning was concerned, was that of defining a draft and simple Software Project Management Model incorporating reuse specific activities/resources/documentation so as to guide the manager in planning reuse activities.

In order to enable an efficient *project tracking* activity, FOR and WITH reuse activities needed to be differentiate from the usual development activities and the effort spent to carry them out during the pilot needed to be collected for further analysis.

A training programme was scheduled to be carried out for the developers consisting in a basic reuse concepts introduction and in an advanced course. The training program was also meant to set the basis for further enactment of reuse within the company and to enable the adequate *staffing* for the reuse experiment.

The reuse initially carried out, was a very fine grained reuse: the components were essentially made up by portions of the logical schema of database applications.

This kind of reuse was made possible by and was very simple because of the use that certain development teams make of CASE tool allowing the automatic generation of portions of the code starting from the logical schema.

Enhancement of reuse studying the possibility of reusing larger portions of the developed systems were deemed appropriate.

Another major issue was that of the possibility of reusing something more than just portions of the schema: associated documentation, test specifications or test cases

No variability analysis was initially carried out and the development of components was not done keeping reuse in mind.

In line with what was said above, guidelines needed to be defined for the development of components which had a better chance to be reused not only within the same application, but in different applications of the same product line and, possibly, across different product lines.

To this respect major attention needed to be paid to the analysis of the variability of the requirements, starting from the requirements of different applications within the same product line to go on with the requirements of applications developed within other product lines.

The main purpose of the work planned in the area of *management of reusable components* was that of defining a suitable model for the components

The preliminary analysis of the specific context carried out during the assessment this report deals with, pointed out the importance of the early and late phases of the software development life-cycle, whereas the coding phase of the development is not considered as crucial. The emphasis on early and late phases needs to be taken into account when defining the component model.

The assessment carried out pointed out that a facet approach to *classification* was appropriate for the specific context. Thus, a preliminary version of a classification schema needed to be defined based on the results of the domain analysis. That is, starting from the facets defined within and suggested by the REBOOT approach, the domain analysis was expected to produce a high level model of the essential items involved in the domain typical applications so as to instantiate the different facets in actual and domain specific values. Furthermore, it was expected to enable the identification of the main characteristics of the developed components again in terms of the facets.

A first selection of *metrics* needed to be chosen so as to make the evaluation of the reusability of a component possible. This selection was to be based upon the results of the domain analysis and of the task in charge of defining the component model.

11.9   Summary of Experiment Results

The RMM assessment was completed and the main objectives, as well as the detailed plan for the pilot were defined.

Furthermore, an initial training was provided to the personnel directly involved in the pilot as well as to other members of the IT department - for a total of 10 persons.

Overall, though the initial schedule of the pilot was not maintained and, at the end of the SER project, only part of the expected results were achieved.

The main reason for the delay in the reuse introduction program was due to the changes at the organisational level that took place in the department where the pilot project was to be carried out.

This, together with the strategic position of the project, lead to the decision of choosing a different pilot, thus delaying the entire enactment process.

Besides the usual observations that can be made about reuse introduction programs, in this case the main error consisted in selecting a strategical project as the basis for introducing reuse in the company. This was mainly an error on the coaching company side, even if, as usual, the coaching company does not have too much leverage on the decision taken by the coached company.

12 Pirelli

- **Consultant Company:** TXT
- **Size of involved team:** 20
- **Domain:** manufacturing
- **Reuse experience:** small
- **Programming language:** C++
- **Type of software:** control software system
- **Scope:** vertical, frameworks
- **Granularity:** O-O frameworks
- **Technology:** REBOOT

12.1 Introduction

Pirelli Informatica (PI) is the corporate I.S. department specifically intended to develop IT strategy and support systems for the manufacturing company Pirelli (PM). Pirelli is structured in two sectors (Tyres and Cables) with about 50 plants world wide.

The similarities among different plants and manufacturing equipment suggest a potential for reuse that had never been investigated thoroughly. On the other hand, the differences existing, as far as the software system requirements of the different sites are concerned, are such that part of the code often needs to be written from scratch.

12.2 Motivation for Reuse

As stated above Pirelli is a company with a number of large factories world-wide. In the Tyre sector, there exist 11 plants located in Europe. All the plants develop similar, but not identical, products and make use of similar, but not identical, manufacturing equipment.

The usual life-cycle of an application encompasses several steps as reproduced in the following:

- development of a system for a pilot site but with requirements generalised through international working groups;
- operation of the system at the pilot site and new release of the system based on the feedback obtained from its operation.
- customisation of the system for a number of other sites;

The customisation process is not trivial due to the differences among plants:

- product related differences due to different requirements on product characteristics;
- manufacturing apparatus differences;
- environmental differences mainly due to the specific way of working and the manufacturing process of each single site;
- cultural differences due to the different technical background of the operators;
- linguistic differences due to the location of the plants.

At the beginning of the experiment reuse was perceived as an opportunity to reduce the costs associated with the customisation of the systems.

12.3 Opportunities

As mentioned in the previous section, reuse is deemed to represent a significant means of cost reduction for the customisation of information systems across different factory sites.

A beneficial side-effect of this "centralised" definition of frameworks was also identified: a through analysis can in fact yield significant results from the point of view of the manufacturing processes. This aspect was also considered from an opposite point of view: reuse-oriented domain analysis studies needed to be carried out in conjunction and in parallel with manufacturing processes analysis studies thus multiplying the benefits as compared to carrying out the two activities in isolation.

Finally, in the long run, potential areas of reuse needed to be sought at even higher level. That is, instead of waiting for a system to be assigned for development to Pirelli Informatica, and then look for potential for reuse, this potential should be analysed and identified at earlier stages in the "business process" in order to optimise the end results and the possibilities of reuse. This last objective was, at any rate, outside the scope of this particular project and it requires further enquiring.

12.4 Experiences

An effort was made prior to the presented project to reuse part of the produced code. The experience was started as a consequence of the introduction of an object-oriented approach to software development and the use of C++ as a programming language. In fact, the development of C++ classes naturally leads to an attempt to reuse the produced code even if in an unstructured way.

The attempt was very limited both as far as its scope and its impact on the actual way of working of the company are concerned. Nonetheless, as a result of this attempt three libraries of components were defined:

- Library of reusable components for the definition of graphical HCI.
- Library of components embodying the access to databases.
- Libraries of components for specific manufacturing process monitoring and control tasks.

All these libraries were not structured in any way and retrieval of software components was not supported by any specific mechanism.

Furthermore, reuse-specific activities were left to the initiative of the individual, no guidelines were defined for the definition of potentially reusable components, that is to maximise the reuse potential of the defined components, and no support system was defined to help developers reuse the available components.

12.5   Target Organisation

As briefly mentioned above this application project was not aimed at changing dramatically the organisational structure of the corporate. Thus, even if organisational and management issues were analysed and taken into account, wider corporate restructuring issues were not dealt with.

Given this hypothesis, the long term objectives of the reuse initiative are described in the following:

- Definition of a repository supporting simple reusable components management procedures such as insertion, deletion, searching. The repository needed to be implemented based on a model of the components to be defined according to the specific development context.
- Definition and enactment of simple procedures taking into account reuse-specific concerns in the software development phases. In particular, both development FOR and development WITH reuse activities were to be defined and integrated in the existing software development life-cycle.

12.6   Major Changes Needed

The changes that were deemed necessary as a first step towards the introduction of reuse at Pirelli Informatica addressed several different areas ranging from the type of software process that needed to be employed at Pirelli to the choice between smaller reusable components and frameworks. In particular, three main goals were set for the project.

First of all, the definition of a process model for the development of software application taking into account reuse-specific activities was needed. Reuse could not be left only and entirely to the initiative of the single developer, but specific and explicit activities should be identified and incorporated in the software development life-cycle at Pirelli.

A parallel improvement of the existing libraries of software components was also considered to be very important. Even if the components available at the beginning of the experiment had not been developed in a systematic reuse-oriented fashion, the possibility of reusing them was greatly hindered by the lack of a structured repository and of a classification schema to facilitate the retrieval of possibly reusable components.

The third major goal of the pilot project, was the definition of a large framework for reuse embracing the concept of generic system framework to be instantiated on the different instances corresponding to different plants. This last objective was set after considering the nature of the manufacturing process whereby continuous processes such as extrusion and mixing of chemical compounds and rubber are performed in different plants by different types of machines.

12.7   Overall Plan

After identifying the major changes needed at the organisational as well as at the technical level, an overall plan was drawn including six major steps: assessment, pilot selection, training, strategy refinement, pilot project implementation, and pilot results analysis. A brief description of their intended scope and rationale, as they were defined at the beginning of the experiment, is provided in the following:

- *Assessment:* Based on the Reuse Maturity Model developed by the REBOOT project, the relevant Key Reuse Areas and Key Reuse Factors shall be analysed. The results of the assessment shall represent the basis for the actual development of a significant pilot project among those carried on within the company.
- *Pilot selection:* Identify pilot with best potential for reuse and representative of the type of applications developed by Pirelli Informatica.
- *Training:* A training program of the personnel involved in the pilot project shall be performed. In particular, it will entail a general introduction to basic reuse concepts and an advanced course on available techniques and technologies.
- *Strategy:* Based on the results of the assessment, define detailed strategy to initiate and enact reuse programme; such a program shall certainly consist of

- a "development for reuse" phase where the main focus shall be on the definition of a general model for the development of S/W systems; in particular, such a model should be the result of a trade-off between generality and convenience. This phase shall also produce a set of reusable components to be used in the instantiation of the general model for different sites;

- a "development with reuse" phase where the main focus shall be on the use and adjustment of the general model of the development of S/W systems. This phase shall also make use, whenever it is judged to be convenient, of the reusable components defined in the previous phase.

• *Pilot project:* A pilot project shall be developed so as to experiment reuse strategies, techniques and to collect relevant data to evaluate the benefits of reuse in the particular context under examination.

• *Pilot result analysis:* Based on the results and data collected during the pilot project, an analysis shall be performed so as to determine the actual benefits introduced by the reuse programme, to identify problems and gaps in the methodology, and to define longer term objectives.

12.8 Experiment Objectives

At the end of the overall plan described in the previous section, a thorough assessment of the Pirelli way of working enabled the definition of detailed objectives for the pilot experiment. In particular, the key reuse areas defined by the REBOOT methodology were analysed and the possible improvement directions identified.

A step by step approach to the introduction of reuse across the company was highly recommended given the fact that the reuse culture within Pirelli Informatica was not widely spread.

A major driver in the selection of the specific projects for the realisation of the experiment and as a start up for the reuse introduction program, was the strategic level within the organisation of the product line the projects were meant to implement. In this context the strategic level of a product indicated the possibility of using the projects results in different factories across Europe rather than using the same product in different departments of the corporate.

The development of reusable components within these projects needed then to be adapted for use in different products of the same line.

A first step towards the assessment of the *cost/pricing* of reuse, was defined to be taken during the development of the pilot project. Even if it was recognised that measurement of costs and benefits concerning reuse was very important, it was not considered to be the focal point of the experiment. The main objective for the application was the experimentation of advanced techniques for the development of reusable frameworks and the assessment of the achievable reuse rate.

It was recognised, nonetheless, that relevant measures needed to be identified and actual data collected during the development. Such measures were meant to provide an indication of the additional costs for developing reusable components (for instance in terms of the time needed to develop them), the time spent in searching for suitable components when developing new applications making use of reusable components and the time spent for adapting reusable components for their use in specific applications.

Further interesting data were identified concerning the improvement in the quality of the developed software with reference to specific quality parameters to be defined based on the specific requirements of the domain under examination.

As far as the *product offer* was concerned, a preliminary domain analysis phase needed to be added to the usual development model so as to collect and study the requirements of the customers/users from more than one site and to elaborate a short-term development strategy for the specific product-line. The need for this preliminary phase of domain analysis was recognised, but considered outside the scope of the experiment to be carried out.

When planning a company wide reuse programme, the dependencies between projects are highly increased. The REBOOT Maturity Model refers in this regard to at least four kinds of *inter-project relationships*:

1. The management of the requirements for the project: the interlocutor is not only the customer but the people in charge of defining the offer for the involved product-line. In the specific case of this pilot this kind of relationship entailed the involvement of different sectors (tyres and cables), of different departments within each sector and of different factory sites. Of course this could only be a long term objective and therefore outside the scope of the specific pilot project under development. Nonetheless, it was during the development of this pilot that the basis to achieve this objectives were to be laid. In particular, it was decided that a first attempt to examine and involve users of similar systems in different sites was to be made.
2. The coordination with the people that have developed the reusable components. This activity needs to be "simulated" during the development of the pilot. That is, there need to be at least one person trying to make used of developed reusable components that did not participate in the development of the reusable components themselves. This individual needed to be in charge of recording all the possible problems encountered in coordinating with the developers of the components for future improvement of this activity. Negotiations should take place between the developers of reusable components and the re-users.
3. The coordination with the reusable components repository manager for the acceptance of the reusable components developed in the project. As for the third type of coordination, a person of the development team needed to be in charge of acting as the repository manager. This role implies in particular the application of quality metrics and classification criteria to the components provided for the insertion in the repository.

Time and resources estimates were deemed necessary as part of the *project planning* activities. A comparison of the actual versus the estimated costs of the pilot in terms of time and resources spent was suggested so as to verify the correctness of the estimates and to add to the knowledge of the company in the field of reuse enactment.

The simple scheme for collecting data concerning project planning in terms of effort and time represented an experimentation in the measurement of a reuse oriented project and the first step towards the definition of more complex schemes to track reuse history within the company. Historical data in fact is the basis for identifying drawbacks in the actual way of enacting reuse. The analysis of the collected data therefore was also suggested to provide indications for the improvement of the reuse-oriented development within Pirelli Informatica.

As far as *staffing* is concerned, it was decided that the necessary competence within the pilot would have been ensured by the planned initial training phase.

Longer term objectives included a permanent training program for the developers involved in reuse-based projects. Furthermore, the personnel that already matured reuse experiences should be involved in these projects so as to increase the possibilities of identifying potential for reuse as well as increasing the reusability of the produced software.

Two main objectives were identified as far as the type of *produced/reused* information is concerned:

1. Widening the scope of reuse defining a more general reusable components model which goes beyond the mere concept of code modules and encompasses higher level descriptions of the system such as requirements specification, design, test specification and test cases, and project documentation. These description are in general called *assets* thus indicating the value of the information enclosed in them. This objective was set in view of an augmented potential for reuse. In fact, on the one hand, the accurate and complete documentation of a software component is an essential means for supporting reuse thus increasing the chances of a developer choosing a component. On the other hand, the more the artefacts of the development process that are reused, the bigger the savings (reusing the design of a software component is better than reusing a few statements of code!).

2. Move from a fine-grained type of reuse to a coarser-grained type of reuse. To this respect, the feasibility of reusing entire sub-systems versus the possibility of reusing entire frameworks should be carefully evaluated based on the specific characteristics of the organisation and of the developed applications. The initial analysis performed during the assessment this report refers to, suggests that there is room for both kinds of coarse-grained reuse and, on this basis the definition of a framework was included among the major changes needed, but a more accurate cost/benefits analysis needs to be performed. This objective, regardless of the type of reusable asset that will be chosen, was set so as to increase the savings achieved in reusing company assets. The feasibility of this objective, furthermore, is suggested by the similarities in the architecture in addition to the similarities in functionalities showed by several applications developed by Pirelli Informatica.

Specific *FOR reuse activities* should be integrated in the software development life-cycle. In particular, system variability analysis and component genericity analysis as well as reuse cost/benefit evaluation shall be added to the "normal" flow of activities.

Specific *WITH reuse activities* should be integrated in the software development life-cycle. In particular, selection criteria for the retrieval of needed components, adaptation guidelines and suggestion for incorporating adapted components shall be added to the "normal" flow of activities.

Adaptation activities are particularly relevant, given the objective defined as far as the type of produced/reused information is concerned.

In fact, if it is true that reusing entire frameworks leads to higher savings, it is also true that the necessary adaptation process becomes more complicated and needs particular attention.

A first version of a simple component model should be defined encompassing the pieces of information that are deemed useful for reusing the stored components. In particular, in addition to maintaining the relationships between a piece of code and the associated development artifacts (e.g., requirement specification, design, test), each software component should also be provided with a set of reuse-specific information: the so called reuse history for example.

A draft and simple *classification* scheme should be defined at the beginning of the pilot as soon as the personnel involved in the project acquired an overall view of the basic concepts pertaining reuse.

The preliminary scheme was thought as being the basis for future improvements and refinements as the knowledge, sensitivity and experience of the developers shall grow.

A prototypical *repository* with basic storage, retrieval and management mechanisms, based on the available technology was deemed necessary so as to support the experimentation of the above mentioned procedures.

A first set of *metrics* enabling to provide a quantitative assessment of a software component should be selected among those available in the literature. The selection process should take into account the specific characteristics of the developed applications.

12.9   Summary of Experiment Results

The experiment was carried out on a pilot project concerning a sub-system of a cable manufacturing process application. In particular, reusable components were re-engineered starting from a normal cables manufacturing application and were re-used in a high tension cables manufacturing application.

In particular, the reusable portions of the application that were identified are listed in the following:

- core product data,
- core process data,
- production orders,
- database access,
- user interface,
- scheduling algorithms,
- GANTT charts.

The reuse rate achieved was around 50% and the remaining 50% of the software needed to be re-implemented. In particular, re-implementation was necessary for

- product and process data in addition to the core one and the necessary access to it;
- orders acquisition interface and warehouse management.

Overall the results of the experiment were satisfactory and the main achievements, besides the savings in term of reused code, encompassed on the one hand immediate results in terms of the definition of reusable components and the development of a repository and, on the other hand, more general achievement in terms of the assessment of reuse feasibility within the company and the spread of a reuse culture.

As far as the development of coarser grained components is concerned, even if the experiment did not go as far as the definition of a general framework, the granularity of the developed components was much coarser and already yielded good percentage savings;

A component repository was set-up based on a first component model definition and supporting a draft classification schema.

The feasibility of fairly high reuse rates was assessed: a 50% reuse rate is a considerable result for the first reuse experiment ever conducted in a structured way and it leads to think that even a higher percentage is within reach.

The development of the experiment together with the training of Pirelli personnel lead to an increased awareness of both the basic reuse concepts and the means necessary to achieve optimal results.

The main problems the project ran into were related to the difficulties encountered in collecting adequate metrics mainly due to the way-of-working within the department. At the end of the experiment, it was recognised that more effort was needed to enforce the collection of relevant metrics. Further investment in this area, both in terms of incentives and in terms of explicit activity definition was therefore needed.

13 Ericsson Radar

- **Consultant Company:** SINTEF
- **Size of involved team:** 30
- **Domain:** radar control
- **Reuse experience:** some
- **Size of application:**
- **Programming language:** ADA, C++,C
- **Type of software:** embedded
- **Scope:** horizontal, common infrastructure
- **Granularity:** general purpose components
- **Technology:** REBOOT

13.1 Introduction

Ericsson Radar is developing software for radar control systems for the military market. Examples of recent projects are software for an artillery hunting radar (tracks trajectory of missiles and computes launch and hit positions), and a simulator for a mobile radar unit which is part of a training simulator for an air defence system.

The main programming language is Ada, but C and C++ is also being used. In addition the development environment include tools for the development of GUI (UIMX, GMS), digital maps (MapLink) and database support (ObjectStore). Recently an Ericsson in-house object oriented analysis and design method called MOOSE has been taken into use. MOOSE builds on OMT [Rum91] and the Paradigm CASE tool is being used to support it. An Ericsson in-house tool is used for configuration and change management.

The development department counts 25 people and is headed by a development manager.

The company started to introduce systematic reuse when they decided to join a SISU project on software reuse[1] in 1991 together with a couple of other companies. SINTEF DELAB participated in the project in the role as provider of reuse expertise

---

[1] SISU is a Norwegian national technology transfer program for the electronics industry, partly funded by the Norwegian research council.

and technology. The contribution of DELAB was strongly influenced by their participation in the REBOOT project.

The SISU project lasted for two years and resulted primarily in reuse learning, the identification of a number of potentially reusable components and the definition of changes to the development organization and process supporting systematic reuse. Initially a pilot project was included but this was postponed due to lack of resources.

A year later the necessary resources were made available to start implementation of the defined measures. Since then four projects have been completed following the modified process. This has resulted in a set of components making up a reusable infrastructure for radar control applications and a significant saving in development effort and elapsed time for the four projects seen as a whole.

The development manager initiated the reuse introduction program and has also acted as *reuse board* and *reuse benefactor*. One developer assisted by one person form the DELAB REBOOT team has acted as reuse *task force* and *reuse agent*[2].

13.2   Motivation for Reuse

There was a trend in military circles towards abandoning the idea that military systems are so special that standard parts does not work, and it was expected that this would pave the way for lower cost systems built from standard parts. At the beginning of the reuse initiative, the transition to a standard target HW and SW platform (UNIX workstations) had already been done in Ericsson Radar, and it was believed that extensive reuse of software parts would be necessary to compete successfully on the future market for military radar control system.

Primarily one was aiming for reduced development cost and time to market without compromising the established level of quality.

13.3   Reuse Experiences and Opportunities

There was little experience with reuse before the start of the SISU project, but there was a growing recognition that there were good opportunities for reuse in the application domain. A number of components of existing systems and ongoing projects were identified as potentially reusable.

The company had a written enterprise model defining standard procedures for development projects, and other important tasks of the organisation. In the outset it did not contain elements that explicitly encouraged reuse, but the existence of a documented model was conceived as a good platform for the enactment of systematic reuse.

---

[2] reuse initiator, reuse board, reuse benefactor, reuse task force and reuse agent are important roles in a reuse introduction process as defined by the REBOOT methodology (see [Karl95])

13.4   Target Reuse Organization

The overall objective was to establish a mode of operation where reuse is a major concern throughout the entire software development process, and where reuse performance is measured and followed up.

13.5   Major Changes

The following major changes were proposed as the first steps towards the goal defined above:

- establish an initial library based on parts of existing software
- adapt the organization and development process for systematic reuse
- define and start to collect quality metrics for components and define a quality model for the library

Below follows a description of how and to which extent these changes have been implemented.

13.5.1   Process

The purely project oriented organization which existed before the reuse initiative was kept, but changes have been introduced in the procedures for initiation, follow up and termination of projects to ensure that reuse is taken into account. This is summarized below:

- The responsibility for coordinating projects lies with the development manager.
- As part of project initiation a contract is set up between the development manager and the project defining project goals and necessary resources, among other things. The contract template has been augmented with parts covering the responsibility of the project for defined reuse goals and a more general responsibility of the project manager to exploit reuse opportunities discovered during the project in cooperation with other projects.
- This has the effect that agreed reuse goals are reflected in the project plans and budgets.
- Project reviews following standard checklists were already established practice, and described in the model. The checklists have been augmented to ensure that reuse goals are followed up.
- Rules has been defined to ensure that marketing people routinely participate in offer preparation and early project reviews with a specific responsibility to ensure that anticipated future requirements are taken into account in the development of reusable components.

13.5.2 Component Library

A standard format for storing reusable components have been defined, requiring that the following types of documentation are stored:

- Requirements specification (large components only)
- Design specification
- Test specification
- Test harness
- Test protocol
- Documentation overview
- Source code
- Make files
- User instruction

In addition it has been decided to maintain a component catalogue containing the following information:

- Component name
- Brief description
- Product no
- Documentation list
- Location
- Where used

An experiment with the REBOOT prototype reuse environment was done, but it was felt that the REBOOT tool environment was an overkill in this early phase in the life of a reuse library.

The current approach is to keep the components in a UNIX file directory structure and maintain a catalogue of components manually. A draft standard for documenting components has been defined.

13.5.3 Quality Assurance

No work has been done so far on measuring and following up component quality.

13.6 Main Results

At the end of the SER project, 4 applications have been completed with the reuse oriented changes described above in effect. This has resulted in the development of 18 reusable components that has been used between 2 and 4 times (including the use in the project that developed the component). In addition two small components from earlier projects were reused in three projects.

The number of uses of each component varies between 2 and 4. Most of the components may be characterized as "global mechanism" components constituting a reusable software infrastructure for radar control applications and covering areas

Table 13.1. Data from Reuse Rrojects (effort given in person months)

	Project 1	Project 2	Project 3	Project 4	Total
# reusable components dev.	10	10	0	0	20
# reused components	3	9	13	12	37
Total effort	250	120	70	60	500
Dev. of reusable comp.	41	30	0	0	71
Appl. specific development	209	90	70	60	429
Saved effort due to reuse	38	43	33	28	142

such as error handling, inter process communication, I/O processing, distribution management, graphic user interface and radar input simulation. There is also a bought in Ada library of standard algorithms and data types, registered as one component

Some cost data from the projects are presented in Table 13.1.

A simple cost-benefit analysis of the reuse introduction program at Ericsson Radar is presented in Fig. 13.1. Already now the program has been profitable, with a net present value of 44 person months[3]. This is about 9% of the total effort on these projects, and about 15% of the total yearly software development effort of the company. The return-on-investment is 180%.

The extra cost for coordinated planning and follow up of projects is not included, but this is considered to be insignificant compared to the development costs.

These components, belonging mainly to a common infrastructure, are expected to be highly reusable in future applications. This is confirmed by the fact that the four applications taking part in this investigation span a wide range of different radar applications. 2 -3 reuses per year for the next years is a realistic assumption. One must expect some costs related to management and maintenance of the components, and this is estimated to 4 person months per year. A cost benefit analysis similar to the one illustrated in Fig. 13.1. but including estimated benefits for the next 3 years based on these assumptions, indicates a net present value of 219 person months.

13.7 Lessons Learned

What it took to achieve the results described above was primarily coordinated planning and follow-up of the four projects and of course the technical insight necessary to identify the common components.

---

[3] Assuming a rate of interest of 10%

Since the benefits were visible within the planning period, funding of the development of reusable components was not really a problem. On the other hand one might say that with more ability to invest before this beneficial situation occurred, one could have developed the components earlier and reduced time to market for the four projects.

The 20 reusable components that have been developed so far implements common needs in the domain, and therefore are little affected by variation in requirements between the applications. Thus representation of variability has not been a problem in the development of these components, and the extra effort to make the components reusable has been relatively low, around 10% for most of the components.

The average reuse rate for the four projects is about 25%. There is still some potential in this type of components, but to achieve significantly higher reuse rates, components more directly related to the radar control functionality must be exploited. These components are likely to be more affected by the variability in the domain and is expected to be more difficult to identify and more costly to make reusable.

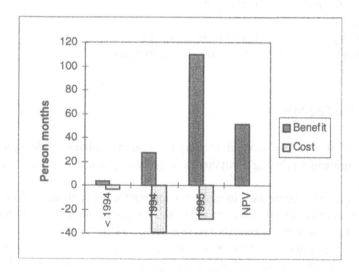

Fig. 13.1. Cost Benefit Analysis (measured in person months)

14 Norsonic

- **Consultant Company:** SINTEF
- **Size of involved team:** 15
- **Domain:** sound measurement instruments
- **Reuse experience:** none
- **Size of application:**
- **Programming language:** C
- **Type of software:** embedded
- **Scope:** vertical
- **Granularity:** application framework
- **Technology:** REBOOT, O-O framework

14.1 Introduction

Norsonic AS is a small Norwegian company that specialises on development, manufacturing and marketing equipment for measuring and monitoring noise and vibrations.

Such equipment is being used in an increasing number of contexts in the modern society as a means to avoid unwanted noise and vibrations, for instance in building acoustics, testing of new car models and monitoring traffic noise.

This variation in use leads to extensive variation in customer requirements both with respect to functionality and physical properties like size, weight and battery lifetime.

So far the company has met this variation by producing a few base models which were replaced by new models at suitable intervals as new technology became available and market needs evolved. The software for a new model was developed from scratch with virtually no reuse of parts from earlier models.

Now the company experiences increased competition, but also a growing market, in particular in the form of new applications of their products. In this situation they are shifting their market strategy towards more emphasis on being able to rapidly produce solutions for new market niches. This means new challenges for the software development department, which are met by adopting systematic reuse.

The reuse program at Norsonic is coached by SINTEF and is based on the REBOOT methodology. It is partially funded by SISU, a national technology transfer program.

14.2 Motivation for Reuse

It is expected that increased reuse of software will bring about the reduction in development cost and time to market for new models necessary to succeed with the new market strategy.

14.3 Reuse Experiences and Opportunities

As mentioned in the introduction previous experience with reuse was very limited, although reuse of code parts by 'copy-and-paste' on an individual basis happened now and then. Normally the reused code was adapted to the new product and there was no recording of what had been reused and what changes were done.

There were no particular provisions to aid the localisation of reusable code. The only way was to ask the other developers if they had developed something similar to what was needed. For this reason, developers mainly reused their own code.

Also there were no recording of the reuse and thus common maintenance of common parts were not exploited.

An initial domain analysis concluded that the application domain was well suited for the application framework approach. The domain analysis was based on REBOOT and PROTEUS guidelines and included a study of existing models, interviews with developers and an assessment of market trends. A conceptual model of the domain that was developed as part of the domain analysis exercise is shown in Fig. 14.1. Although developed independently, the software of existing instrument models exhibit many similarities and it is expected that around 50% of the planned framework will be parts adapted from existing instruments

14.4 Major Changes

An assessment of the current development organisation based on the REBOOT reuse maturity model was performed and goals were set for the different key reuse factors. Based on this assessment the following major needs for change were identified:

- Develop a common architectural framework for sound measurement instruments.
- Build a library of components populating the framework, with appropriate alternatives where this is necessary to cover existing and anticipated variation in requirements and technology.

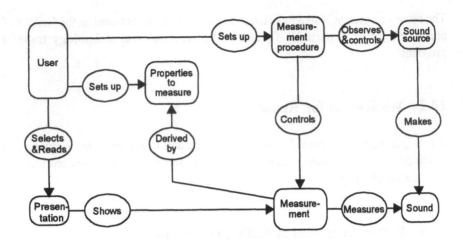

Fig. 14.1. Conceptual Model of Noise Measurement Domain

- Adapt the organisation to facilitate better communication between projects and better coordination of projects towards common long term goals.
- Rigorise the development process and incorporate consideration of reuse opportunities and opportunities for developing new reusable components in all phases of development.
- Introduce a configuration management scheme for managing the sharing of components between instruments..

A two year plan was set up to implement these changes with a personnel budget of two person years.

14.5 Results

At the time of writing the following results have been achieved:

- An initial proposal for the common application architecture has been defined. It divides the software into 7 major technical subdomains or component groups.
- A domain oriented organisation, based on this breakdown, has been adopted and teams have been set up for each subdomain. Each team will be responsible for developing and maintaining reusable components covering the needs of development projects in their subdomain.
- In order to ensure communication between the subdomain teams and market people, so-called specification groups have been defined. A specification group includes market people working in a particular market segment and developers from the most relevant technical teams, and is responsible for defining current and future requirements of that segment.
- A regular meeting of project managers has been introduced to handle inter project planning and coordination.

- The development process and accompanying roles has been redefined.
- An initial solution for the library has been implemented. The library consists of a file catalogue structure. Each component has a header file in a standard format. The individual files constituting a component is packed into a zip file. Search for components is supported by a component catalogue file produced by concatenating all the header files.

14.6 Lessons Learned

These initial solutions are now being applied and refined in a pilot project. It is too early to draw final conclusions, but below we summarise some observations made so far:

- The purely project oriented organisation of the development department was held responsible for the low degree of reuse in an application domain with inherently good opportunities for reuse.
- The experience with practicing the new organisation in the requirements definition and planning for the pilot project is generally positive. It is felt that the involvement of the component teams in the estimation and planning has lead to better plans.
- A requirements template has been developed, containing stable requirements and slots for varying requirements. For the pilot project the varying requirements (i.e. requirements particular for that application) make up only 20-30% of the text of the requirements specification. This is consistent with experience from other application frameworks.
- Concerning the reuse library aspect, the simple scheme that has been proposed appears to be sufficient, considering the size of the organisation and the well bounded application domain. However it is clear that the sharing of components that reuse will bring about will require more sophisticated configuration management procedures than what is currently practiced, and probably tool support.

15 Telecom Company

- **Consultant Company:**   EP-Frameworks
- **Size of involved team:**
- **Domain:**   Telecom network management
- **Reuse experience:**   Some
- **Size of application:**   50 KLOC
- **Programming language:**
- **Type of software:**   Data gathering, processing and reporting
- **Scope:**   product line, emphasis on application domain
- **Granularity:**   Application framework
- **Technology:**   REBOOT

15.1 Introduction

This experiment focused on the introduction of the application framework approach in the domain of management systems for telecommunications networks. Such systems support tasks like statistics gathering, charging and fault management.

The company operates worldwide and have to cope with differences in standards and regulations between different markets. So far this had been tackled by separate development organisations for the main markets. Each development organisation developed and maintained their own product line of applications for the main tasks of network management. Corresponding applications in different product lines offered the same main functionality, but were different because they adhered to different standards and regulations. This is illustrated in Fig. 15.1.

Some reuse of common components had been exploited, but this did not give the reduction in time-to-market and improved quality that the company strived for.

15.2 Motivation for Reuse

The company needed to reduce the time-to-market for new applications and to improve the quality. Development cost was not so critical. Earlier reuse of basic common components did not bring about the needed results and a more comprehensive reuse strategy was therefore sought for.

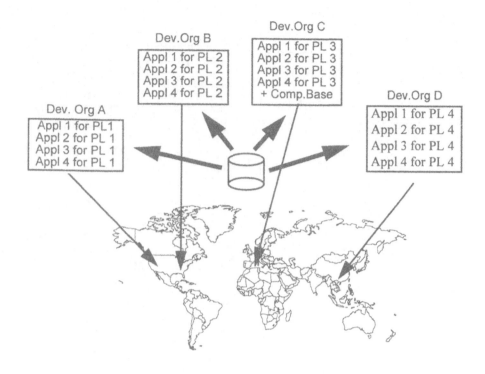

Fig. 15.1. The Initial Development Organisation

The characteristics of the application domain indicated that the object oriented application framework approach would be feasible and that this approach had the potential to provide the needed improvements.

15.3   Reuse Experiences and Opportunities

The company already had some experience with reuse prior to the project. A common collection of components supporting basic communication with the network element had been developed and reused across applications and product lines for some time. In addition there were some 3rd party products, e.g. a database manager and a class library for building user interfaces. This is called the "base of components" in this document. This base of components is mature and are widely used, mainly because the application projects are forced to use it.

In addition to the reuse of the common basic components, ad hoc copy-and paste reuse happened occasionally when the same developers were involved in two product lines. Finally there were some ad hoc reuse of results from the early phases between applications of the same application type, for instance reuse of requirement specifications for the common main functionality.

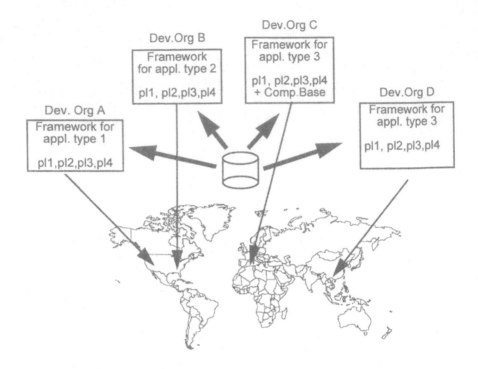

Fig. 15.2. The Developments Organisation Adapted for Application Framework Reuse

Despite the marked differences due to different standards and regulations, corresponding applications from the different product lines still exhibited a high degree of similarities, and in the cases that ad hoc reuse had taken place it had been successful. Therefore it was it was believed that significantly higher reuse rates could be achieved by generating corresponding applications from a common application framework.

Since he applications of a certain application type, had been developed by different teams, there were many more differences than the different standards and regulations required.

15.4   Target Reuse Organisation

The responsibilities of the developments organisations was shifted such that instead of being responsible for a product line as before, each organisation became responsible for one or more application types and their adaptation for the different markets. In this way each development organisations is given an area of responsibility that it is natural to serve with one or more application frameworks.

The market organisation continued to be divided according to the product lines. This is illustrated in Fig. 15.2.

The initial instantiations of the frameworks covered by this experiment were done by the framework developers, but this may be done by pesonnel associated with the product line in the future.

15.5 Major Changes Needed

In addition to changing the responsibilities of the development organisations as described above, a major task was to re-educate the development staff to focus on building application domain knowledge for a limited set of applications rather that overall market knowledge. To support this shift, and establish the contact of each development organisation with the different markets, a reference group for each application type and was established, with a responsibility to assist the development organisation in charge to evolve the application domain knowledge in accordance with the needs of the markets.

Furthermore the staff had to learn how to build object oriented application frameworks. Although some staff members had good knowledge of object oriented programming, they lacked experience in building application frameworks.

15.6 Overall Plan

Improvements of the development process (including reuse), is an ongoing activity within all parts of the organisation. Due to hard pressure from the market and a general shortage of experienced and good developers, it is impossible to perform pilot projects or investigations that incorporate the developers. Most reuse experiments and studies must therefore be performed in ordinary projects, which are very sceptic to introducing something that may require extra effort and that causes additional risks.

The development of the initial application frameworks were done along with their first instantiation by the ordinary development staff, but a couple of external experts or reuse and object-orientation were provided to assist each development team.

15.7 Main Results

This report was produced after application frameworks for three application types had been developed and one of them had been instantiated for two markets. Some cost data for the framework for which reuse experience exists is presented below:

- developing one application along with a framework costs 1.4 times the cost of classical development;

- developing two applications along with a common reusable framework costs 1.75 times the cost of classical development;
- developing further applications using the framework reduces to 0.35 times the cost of development from scratch;
- by involving managers and engineers to plan and carefully engineer the reuse aspect of the work, casual reuse was eliminated - thus improving quality and reducing cost of repair activity.

Other observations worth mentioning are

- The frameworks include work products from all development phases. There are product plans and product structures that support the frameworks and the work of increasing the reuse potential is continuing.
- Developing the framework along with the first instantiation, as was the case in this experiment, led to low up-front investment and an acceptable extra load on the development organisation.
- Several developers has succeeded in learning the techniques for developing a framework, however the incentive for using them may sometimes be low because of lack of knowledge.
- When developing these first application frameworks, some parts of the existing applications were reused. However the experience from this type of reuse is not very positive. Generally significant rework of the reused parts were necessary to make them usable in the framework and the programmers felt that in most cases it would have been less work to develop these parts from scratch.
- Some of the design and coding guidelines associated with the object oriented application framework approach conflicts with traditional wisdom, and therefore sometimes were hard to accept.

16 Telecom Gateway Framework

- **Consultant Company:**   Frameworks
- **Size of involved team:**   small
- **Domain:**   gateways
- **Reuse experience:**   small
- **Size of application:**
- **Programming language:**
- **Type of software:**   embedded
- **Scope:**   vertical
- **Granularity:**   O-O framework
- **Technology:**   REBOOT

16.1 Introduction

The operation of telecommunication networks involves collecting and analysing data from and tuning of a number of network elements (for instance switches). A number of administrative applications exists to support these activities, but the interaction between such applications and the network elements they manage is not very efficient today. For instance collecting data from the switches is typically done by storing the data on tapes in each local site, and then transporting the tapes to a central site for analysis.

The purpose of a gateway is to serve as a mediator between the administration systems and the network elements that present a uniform abstract interface to both sides and performs the necessary translations. This is illustrated in Fig. 16.1. The introduction of gateways will lead to simplification in the administrative applications by freeing them from keeping track of the peculiarities of the different types of networks elements, as well as to automation of data collection from the network elements. This means more efficient operation of the telecommunication networks and there is therefore a strong interest in the market for such products.

In Ericsson the need for gateways had been realised and one gateway product had been developed. Then to further exploit this market, Ericsson decided to develop Cafka, an application framework for gateways intended to serve as the basis for a number of different gateway products. This report discusses technical issues

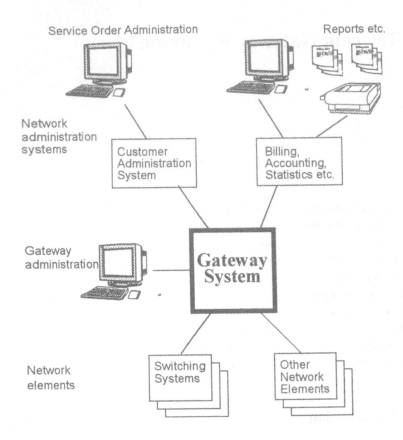

Fig. 16.1. Context Diagram for the Telecom Gateway Application

concerning the development of the framework and presents preliminary results after the first instantiation.

A project team was assembled for the job with substantial experience in reuse oriented software development from earlier projects.

16.2   Motivation for Reuse

There are many different networks on the market today with different switches, different communication protocols etc. Therefore there is a need for a number of different but still similar gateways. The commonality between them is expected to be sufficient that both substantial savings and significantly shortened time-to-market can be achieved by exploiting software reuse.

16.3   Framework Development

Given the characteristics of the application domain presented above, the application framework approach was a natural choice, and the object oriented application framework paradigm was taken as a model.

16.3.1 Domain Modelling

The first step towards the realisation of the framework was to develop a conceptual model of the gateway domain. This was done using the group dynamic modelling technique [Kar95]. This technique differs from ordinary modelling techniques in that domain knowledge is not captured in interviews, but rather by bringing together the people that are knowledgable in the domain or otherwise expected to be in close contact with the system, in common modelling sessions. The major advantage of this approach is that consensus is focused and therefore chances to reach a common understanding of the domain is better. During the Group dynamic modelling sessions, the model was expressed using a simple graphic notation with the following elements:

- concepts
- properties of concepts
- specialisation of concepts
- relationships between concepts
- comments.

16.3.2 Analysis, Design and Implementation

In the following analysis and design phases, the domain model was formalised and detailed using OMT [Rum91] and implemented in C++. This work was directed by the reuse guidelines of REBOOT. The design guidelines were found to be particularly useful. For instance guidelines like the "top of a class hierarchy should be abstract" and "use pointers to abstract base classes", significantly improved the reusability of the framework.

Abstract classes were used extensively to cater for the perceived variation in the domain. An instantiation in several steps was foreseen, dictated by the structure of the anticipated variation of requirements in the gateway domain. The domain includes administration systems for billing, for customer administration, for service ordering etc. Each of these systems are typically customized for different markets. The root framework implements properties common to all gateways. Then there will be sets of related specialisation for a particular category of administration system or for a particular market. Building and maintaining partially instantiated framework incorporating such sets of related specialisations may speed up application development considerably. This is illustrated in Fig. 16.2.

The resulting application framework consists of

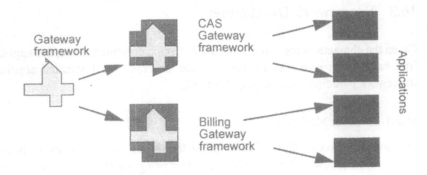

Fig. 16.2. Specialization of the Cafka Gateway Framework

- The conceptual domain model
- OMT analysis models
- OMT design models
- Code components
- Programmers guide

The programmers guide explains how to handle new or modified requirements when instantiating the framework in the areas of variation that were foreseen during the development of the framework.

Only one general component, that is a component reusable outside the framework, was developed, namely a string class. All the other components were intimately coupled to the framework and not conceived as reusable in other contexts.

16.4   Instantiating the Framework

The first instantiation of the framework was done to develop a gateway for the Ericsson MD 110 telephone exchange. This included development of the following components:

- RS232 and X.25 communication
- socket communication
- MD 110 specifics
- user interface
- INGRES database interface and database schemas

These components are expected to be reusable in future instantiations of the framework, for instance to create gateways for other network elements, or to create MD 110 gateways for other contexts. However, since the components specialize classes of the framework, they will not be easily reusable in other environments. A few minor shortcomings of the framework were identified, but the necessary extensions amounted to less than one percent (less than 100 lines out of the total of 10 Klines constituting the framework).

16.5 Main Results

Some data from the framework development and first instantiation is presented in Table 16.1. The reuse rate derivable from these data is 37%, which is rather modest for an application framework. However, what is counted as instantiation code in this first instantiation, also include the development of several components expected to be reusable in future instantiations of the framework.

This product family represents the most beneficial business within the company today. The short time-to-market and the flexibility are the key success factors and are a result of software reuse with the object oriented application framework approach. The framework itself is today divided into several smaller frameworks. Products being released in new versions of the framework still keep the approach together although parts of the framework changes.

Table 16.1. Data from the First Instantiation of the Cafca Gateway Framework

Item	Value
Size of framework code	10 KLOC
Cost of framework development	350 persondays
Size of instantiation code	17 KLOC
Cost of framework instantiation	250 persondays
Cost of developing gateway from scratch[a]	750 persondays

[a.] Estimated

16.6 Lesson Learned

The project started directly with the approach of developing a framework and using the framework to develop products. Since a new organisational structure was set up for the gateway products, there was no existing organisational structure to adapt for reuse. Therefore the experiences primarily relate to the technical aspects of application framework development and use.

The most important success factors were:

- very competent designers,
- extensive domain knowledge,
- flexible architecture.

Developing the framework in parallel with the first application with the same manager responsible for both, lead to a good balance between generality and ease of instantiation, and good support for rapid application development.

The initial development was an investment from the company until a customer ordered the first product. From then on the business itself financed further development. The start must always be an investment, but as soon as possible, there should be a customer project, in order to develop something that the customer wants.

Finally some good advice:

- Do not discuss the framework approach or the technical solutions with the customers, they will be confused. Talk about time-to-market and flexibility and then sell good applications with a good profit instead.
- Try to find simple solutions, simple organizational models and simple economic models.

Acronyms

CMM	Capability Maturity Model
ER	Ericsson Radar
ESI	European Software Institute
GSFC	NASA / Goddard Space Flight Center
HCI	Human Computer Interface
HP	Hewlett-Packard
IL	Instrumentation Laboratory
IS	Information System(s)
IT	Information Technology
KLOC	Thousand Lines Of Code
NPV	Net present value
OMT	Object Modelling Technique
O-O	Object Oriented
PCL	Proteus Configuration Language
RBO	Reusable Business Object
RMM	Reuse Maturity Model
SER	Software Evolution and Reuse
WWW	World Wide Web

References

[Bas96]   Basili, V.R. et. al.: *How Reuse Influences Productivity in Object-oriented Systems*. Communications of the ACM 39:10, 104-116 (1996)

[Bel87]   Belkhatir, N., Estublier, J.: *Experience with a Data Base of Programs*. ACM SIGPLAN Notices 22:1, 84-91 (1987)

[Bel95]   Bennett, K.: *Legacy Systems: Copying with success*. IEEE Software 12:1, 19-23 (1995)

[Big87]   Biggerstaff, T. and Richter, C.: Reusability Framework, Assessment, and Directions. *IEEE Software* 4:2, 41-49 (1987)

[Bræ93]   Bræk, R. and Haugen, Ø.: Engineering Real Time Systems. Prentice Hall 1993

[Fel79]   Feldman, S. I.: Make, A Program for Maintaining Computer Programs. Software - Practice and Experience 9:4, 255-265 (1979)

[Fav90]   Favaro, J.: *What Price Reusability*. In Proceedings of the First Symposium on Environments and Tools for Ada. New York: ACM 1990, pp. 115-124

[Fen94]   Fenton, N et. all., Science and substance: A Challenge to Software Engineers, IEEE Software 11:3, 86-95 (1995)

[Flo95]   Floch, J.: PCL and PCL toolset evaluation at GAREX. PROTEUS consortium, Trondheim, Technical report P-WP-A131b-JF211-SIN.02, August 1995

[Flo96]   Floch, J.: *Enabling Reuse with a Configuration Language*. In: Proceedings of Fourth International Conference on Software Reuse, Orlando 1996. Los Alamitos, IEEE Computer Society Press1996, pp. 176-185

[Fra94]   Frakes,W. B. and Isoda, S.: *Success Factors for Systematic Reuse*, IEEE Software 11:5, 14-19 (1994)

[Gam94]   Gamma et. al.: *Design Patterns Elements of Reusable Object-Oriented Software*. Reading, MA: Addison-Wesley 1994

[Gor91]   Gorman, J. and Johansen, U.: *Engineering the Implementation of SDL Specifications*. In: Færgemand, O. and Reed, R. (eds.): SDL '91 Evolving Methods *Proceedings of the Fifth SDL Forum*, Glasgow 1991. Amsterdam: North Holland 1991, pp. 367-378

[Gul95]   Gulla, B. and Gorman, J.: *Supporting Evolution of SDL-based Systems: Industrial Experience*. In: Bochman, G. V., Dssouli, R. and Rafiq, O.: *Proceedings of the 8th International IFIP conference on Formal Description Techniques for Distributed Systems and Communications Protocols (FORTE'95)*, Montreal 1995. London: Chapman & Hall 1995, pp. 253-268

[ITU93]   Specification and Description Language SDL. Recommendation Z.100, CCITT ITU, Geneva, Switzerland 1993

[Jon94]   Jones, C.: *Assessment and Control of software risks.* Yourdon Press Comput-
             ing Series, 1994
[Kar95]   Karlsson, E. A.: *Software Reuse: A Holistic Approach.* Wiley Series in Soft-
             ware Based Systems, 1995
[Kru92]   Krueger, C. W.: Software Reuse. *ACM Computing Surveys* 24:2 (1992)
[Lim94]   Lim, W. C.: *Effects of Reuse on Quality, Productivity and Economics,* IEEE
             Software 11:5, 23-30 (1994)
[Mar91]   Margono, J. and Lindsey, L.: *Software Reuse in the Air Traffic Control Ad-
             vances Automation System.* In Proceedings of the Software Reengineering
             and Reuse Conference, Nat'l Inst. for Software Quality and Productivity,
             Washington, D. C., 1991
[Pro93]   Hewlett Packard and Matra Marconi Space and Cap Gemini Innovation: *Do-
             main Analysis Method.* Proteus Deliverable D3.2A, October 1993
[Pro94]   PCL-V2 Reference Manual. Proteus consortium, Technical Report P-DEL-
             3.4.D-1.9, September 1994.
[Pro95]   Proteus framework. Proteus Consortium, Technical Report P-DEL-3.5.A.2.0,
             February 1995
[Ram96]   Ramachandran M. and Fleischer, W.: *Design for Large Scale Software Re-
             use: An Industrial Case Study,* to be presented at the Fourth International
             Conference on Software Reuse, Orlando 1996. Courtesy of the authors.
[Ree95]   Reenskaug, T. et. al.: Working with Objects - The OORAM Software Engi-
             neering Method. Prentice Hall 1995
[Rum91]   Rumbaugh, J: Object-oriented Modelling and Design. Prentice Hall 1991
[SER95]   *Solutions for Software Evolution and Reuse.* The SER Consortium, SER De-
             liverable SER-D2-A, September 1995
[SDT95]   SDT User Manual, TeleLOGIC Malmö AB Sweden.
[SPR94]   Jones, C.: *Becoming "Best in Class": the Path to Software Excellence.* from
             the Knowledge Base of the Software Productivity and Research WWW Ser-
             ver, http://www.spr.com
[Tas]   OOram User Manual. Taskon, Oslo.
[Tic85]   Tichy, W. F.: RCS - A System for Version Control. *Software - Practice and
             Experience,* 15:7, 637-654 (1985)
[Try95]   Tryggeseth, E. and Gulla, B. and Conradi, R.: Modelling Systems with Vari-
             ability using the PROTEUS Configuration Language. In: Estublier, J. (edi-
             tor): *Proceedings of the Fifth International Workshop on Software Configu-
             ration Management,* Seattle WA. Lecture Notes in Computer Science, Vol.
             1005. Berlin: Springer-Verlag 1995, pp. 216-240
[TST95]   TST User Manual. Telox, Norway